inscriptions for headstones

essays by matthew vollmer

OUTPOST
19

Outpost19 | San Francisco
outpost19.com

Vollmer, Matthew,
            Inscriptions for Headstones / Matthew Vollmer.
            ISBN 9781937402372 (pbk)
            ISBN 9781937402389 (ebook)

Cover photo and design by Brandon Buckner.

Library of Congress Control Number: 2012946432

OUTPOST
19

also by Matthew Vollmer

Future Missionaries of America

*Fakes: An Anthology of Pseudo-Interviews,
Faux Lectures, Quasi-Letters, "Found" Texts, and Other
Fraudulent Artifacts*
(co-editor)

acknowledgements

some of these epitaphs appeared under different nu-merals at *Carolina Quarterly, The Collagist, Dark Sky Magazine, DIAGRAM, elimae, fringe magazine, Ghost Town, Hayden's Ferry Review, LUMINA, PANK, Passages North, Phoebe,* and *The Pinch Journal.*

this book was completed
in part
by a grant
from the National Endowment
for the Arts

for KP & EV

"I die daily."
St. Paul, 1 Corinthians 15:31

"I am large. I contain multitudes."
Walt Whitman, "Song of Myself"

inscriptions for headstones

matthew vollmer

I

here lies a man who felt compelled to visit time and time again the house where
he'd spent the majority of his childhood;
a house that his parents had built above
the intersection of two creeks in a shadowy cove in the westernmost tip of North
Carolina; a house made of wood and
stone with a sixteen-windowed room
on one side that let in the sun and over-
looked a rhododendron thicket; a house
that smelled often of oranges and bak-
ing bread and the deceased's mother's
perfume; a house whose three unfolding
bathroom mirrors could open a corridor
into infinity; a house whose vents the
deceased inspected for lost toys, staring
down the oblivion-dark holes as metal-
lic-smelling wind stung his eyes; a house
that figured in one of the deceased's re-
curring dreams, in which he rose from a
manger (less delusions of grandeur than
an obsession with nativity scenes) and
watched as a 16mm movie of his home

was projected onto a screen, a magical window through which he then vaulted himself, landing upon the mossy, mole-rutted front yard, which he climbed, then up the concrete stairs and through the house with its dark wood banister and upside-down yellow wallpaper and through the kitchen, and onto the back porch, where he found his mother dancing in a wedding dress; a house which, after his parents had procured a larger and wilder swathe of land in a more remote location, they'd sold to an older woman and her husband (a scientist who had at one time worked for NASA), though it turned out that this man was unkind and perhaps abusive and the woman herself believed the house to be haunted, a claim that the deceased found beguiling, as he could recall zero instances of anything even remotely related to phantasmagoric activity, though the deceased and his sister had, as kids, engineered their own makeshift haunted houses, hanging tarps from the ceilings to create passageways, lighting candles, smearing their faces with a mixture of bananas and red food coloring, tying semitransparent dental floss to old coolers and pulling the strings when visitors walked by, thus revealing the decapitated bodies of dolls, or throwing a wig out of the dark space beneath the stairs, which was supposedly a cave where a crazy woman scalped people, and of course none of this was nearly as scary as the deceased liked to think, and their house was not really haunted, at least that's what they thought, because the current owner was insisting that there must be a spirit or two in the house, because both she and her husband had witnessed cupboards and doors opening and closing by themselves, had heard something walking upon the floor above them when they knew no one was there, a series of events that had lead the woman to decide to contact whatever it was that had been making these noises, and so, one night, when she was alone in the house, she'd turned out the lights and lit candles and incense and laid herself down on the couch (the one in the living room, beside the indoor relaxation fountain that trickled eternally) and said, "Okay, whatever or whoever you are, make yourself known," and then, the door to the attic—which, once upon a time, had been a place that the deceased, as a boy, had almost never entered by himself and whose pink insulation and old mothballed clothes and big hefty trunks had pretty much creeped him out—began throwing itself open and then slamming itself shut, an activity that had caused the woman to yell "Please! Stop!" and the door stopped and she felt exhilarated and also quite frightened but now knew for sure there was a spirit living there and somehow—the deceased would not be able to remember what, exactly, the woman did, though she had shown him a photograph of her aura, had pointed out a green spot on the halo at about five o'clock that she claimed signified paranormal activity—it was ascertained that this particular spirit was a Native American girl who had been buried on the same site as the house and that she had never been given an adequate funeral, so the woman performed some sort of ritual and things returned—more or less—to normal, though her husband moved to San Diego and now the woman lived in the house all by herself and once a year the deceased would go back and take a tour of the place where he'd lived and think how small this house was and how different it looked now that the wallpaper had been torn off and how sweet the basement was now that the woman had turned it into a meditation room, and how lonely the house seemed now without all the stuff that the deceased remembered had once been there, and which he would superimpose onto the rooms with his mind, wondering each time he came why he subjected himself to what—in the end—was always a depressing sort of exercise, and couldn't he be said to be a kind of ghost himself, an entity who haunted a house that was no longer his but always would be a place that no longer recognized him, a home that had died, and that came to life only in dreams

II

rest in eternal slumber boy for whom the
bathtub had become a kind of crucible-
stage upon which the deceased would
enact a range of private melodramas, one
of which involved plugging the drain
and turning the shower nozzle on full
blast and pretending that he was slosh-
ing through a flood and that the wall of
the tub was not, in fact, a fiberglass shell
but the outer hull of Noah's Ark and that
he—that is, the deceased—had been one
of the people who'd refused to believe
that such a flood was coming, in part
because—as a citizen of the antediluvi-
an and thus rain-free world, where, according to Genesis, a mist rose from the
ground to water the earth every morning—he had never before seen rain, and
in part because Noah had been predict-
ing this rain for as long as the deceased
could remember, the man couldn't shut
up about it, and nobody but Noah's
otherwise ostracized family so much as

gave a second thought as to whether the old man's ravings contained a shred of truth, but now here it was, a deluge so astounding, so relentless the deceased could barely breathe, much less walk, an utterly debilitating downpour, plus he was naked, maybe because he'd ripped off his robe (assuming pre-flood people wore robes, when—who knows—they might've been as technologically and fashionably advanced a culture as to wear pants and shirts and sneakers and digital waterproof watches), shredding it as an expression of grief and/or terror and/or gnashing of teeth and/or because the fabric had been weighing him down as he sought higher ground or to keep up with the Ark as it began to float away, the outer shell of which the man—i.e., the deceased—was now pounding, his fists striking the now rainslickened gopher wood, begging Noah to please give him another chance, he believed now, he could see the error of his ways, he should've listened, etc., so please open the door, an act that Noah—regardless of whether or not he could hear the man's cries—would've been utterly powerless to perform, as the opening of the Ark's door happened on G-D's watch, and would be carried out by one of His angels, but not until the Earth had been washed clean of all its wicked people, a group to which the deceased would now pretend to realize he belonged, thinking, *I am one of the wicked* and *I am going to die*, and had you been there to witness the boy as he performed this imaginative exercise, and if you had asked him why he felt compelled to make believe that he was one of the lost, he wouldn't have been able to explain, though years later he might guess that maybe he simply felt sorry for and sympathized with the people who hadn't believed Noah's message, and that he—the deceased—understood that the chances were fairly high, were he to have been alive during Noah's time, that he wouldn't have made it into the Ark, and moreover that he would've most likely laughed at the old man, because, let's face it, the deceased often laughed and made fun of people, especially those who were different or odd, like the little frog-faced man at church with the tiny round glasses, or the serious and mustachioed and diminutive German man who sold a so-called miracle nutritional supplement called Barley Green and always dedicated hymns he played on his violin to his mother, or the corpse-faced ex-pastor who'd slink forward post-benediction to inflict long-winded announcements about Stop Smoking clinics and Walk-a-Thons, all of whom the deceased had imitated or mocked at some time or other, so why should he think he wouldn't also have laughed at Noah, a man who'd built out of pitch and gopher wood what must've seemed like the most absurd structure ever devised, but not only that, the man had worked on it not for one year or two years or ten or twenty, but an entire *century*, which, if you thought about it, seemed like an insane amount of time for a man and his three sons to be working on anything, even if the Ark itself was three stories tall and as long as 36 tennis courts, but maybe they—meaning Noah and his sons— were slow or exceedingly deliberate or just downright inept and don't forget that Noah, in a future story, turns out to be the kind of guy who gets drunk and passes out naked in his tent, so maybe he wasn't the finest or best or most productive carpenter, but whatever, it didn't matter now, it was too late, the rains had come and the door had been sealed shut, just as another metaphorical door would be shut during the End of Time, when, in the Heavenly Sanctuary, after Jesus Christ had gone through the books—billions and billions of books, each one containing the transcription of the life of a particular human being: all the thoughts and actions and perceptions and interactions that this person's recording angel had chronicled, perhaps using a feather plucked from a heavenly peacock and dipped into an inkwell made of 24-carot gold—and after the Son of G-D had decided who were to be called Home, no more sinners would be able to repent, the lost would be the lost, the saved would be the saved, and a Time of Trouble would be unleashed upon the earth, a series of plagues that'd include boils and the sea turning to blood and the sun scorching the flesh of those who'd worshipped— inadvertently or not—the Beast, and though those who'd kept G-D's Law would remain unscathed, they'd have to suffer their own particular slings and arrows, as they could count on being hunted down by the armies of the Antichrist, a future scenario which the family of the deceased often referred to as the time when they would have to "flee to the mountains," wondering—sort of wistfully—how G-D would protect them and where they might go and whether or not invisible force-fields would be placed around them, a scenario that troubled the deceased, because what if he wasn't ready, what if he hadn't repented before that sanctuary door closed, what if he, like the man he was pretending to be right now, just gave up, and let himself fall headfirst into a flood, how long he could go without breathing, what dreams would he have, what hallucinations, and what it would feel like to realize, just before he lost consciousness, that he was utterly and irreversibly doomed

III

rest in peace man who refused to think of
himself as a thief but who could, supposing the conditions were right, justify the
taking of things that were not his, and
who, as a thirteen-year-old boy visiting
the mall during his annual pilgrimage
from the mountains of North Carolina
to the bustling metropolis of Greenville,
South Carolina, where he would seek
out Air Jordan high tops and severely
tapered Bugle Boy stonewashed jeans
and mock turtlenecks and checkered
cardigans, once found an excuse to part
ways with his mother to visit the mall's
only bookstore—a Waldenbooks on the
first level—where he began nonchalantly browsing the periodicals, flipping
through an issue of *MAD* that lampooned
a Cosby Show spinoff, skimming a *Sports
Illustrated* and noting the "Faces in the
Crowd," glancing every now and again
toward the cashier—a short, squat woman with big round lenses, braided hair,

and loose beige clothing—then back toward the top shelf, where, in prophylactic sacks, a host of magazines bearing titles in lurid colors—*OUI* and *CHERI* and *CLUB*—waited patiently for him to make his move, except that today he wouldn't have to make as much of a move as he'd anticipated, having realized, after picking up a *Rolling Stone*, that somebody who'd come before him must have been struck by a similar idea, namely the selecting of a title from the above treasury of smut and sliding it inside another magazine, thus granting the illusion that the reader was looking, not at *Penthouse Forum*, but at *Better Homes & Gardens*, though in this case, the magazine-within-in-a-magazine had been the exact issue the deceased had been hoping to find, namely the September issue of *Playboy*, an issue which was of great interest as it featured a woman named Jessica Hahn, a woman the deceased had seen on TV and then in the pages of *People* and *Time* magazines, a woman who had claimed that the televangelist Jim Bakker—husband of weepy, raccoon-eyed Tammy Faye—had raped and devirginized her, then paid her upwards of 250K hush money, and because Jim and Tammy Faye, at the time, had built up a multimillion-dollar Christian broadcasting company and were quite famous, and because Jessica Hahn's allegations had basically ripped apart an enterprise that any thinking person would've deemed hypocritical and money-grubbing, and because Jessica Hahn was, by conventional standards, quite beautiful (many would use the word "hot"), she was subsequently contacted by *Playboy* to pose nude, because people liked scandals—especially those of a sexual nature—and because it's one thing to see an anonymous woman naked, and quite another thing to see a famous or even semi-famous woman naked, and because this magazine knew it could capitalize upon the idea of Jessica Hahn taking back her sexuality—taking charge of it, as it were—by undressing in a studio and exposing her bare breasts and bare arms and bare legs and bare buttocks but never her bare sex, always positioning herself so at least that part of her was hidden or draped with a stain sheet or the corner of a robe, and Jessica Hahn had—like Vanessa Williams and Vanna White before her, two other semi-famous women that the deceased had been curious to see without clothes, part-

14

ly because magazines like Time and People had published portions of these hazy, soft-core pictures from the magazines in which they'd originally appeared—said yes and she had posed nude, the photographic evidence of which the deceased was now eyeballing, his heart pumping wildly, staring with disbelief at the sight of this woman who he didn't know but who he had heard interviewed on TV, who he had seen footage of on the news, and now here she was, right in front of him: a kid who was too young to actually buy the magazine and would've been far too embarrassed to try even if he hadn't been, so instead he slapped the *Rolling Stone* shut and pretended to give the news stand one last look, as if to say, Yeah, I guess I'm done with this section, then moseyed past the cashier, past a table stacked with copies of *Silence of the Lambs* and *Queen of the Damned*, past *A Brief History of Time* and *The Satanic Verses*, down to the Self-Help section, i.e., the next-to-last aisle, where he squatted and, eye level with *All I Ever Really Needed to Know I Learned in Kindergarten*, opened the magazine, and, with feverish hands, flipped to the Hahn section, carefully ripping out the page upon which she had reclined upon a twisted and shimmering bed of satin sheets, frantically folding this into quarters, which he then slid into his pocket, afterwards placing the magazine behind a bookshelf, his face slick with sweat, worrying that secret cameras had recorded him, and that a man monitoring these cameras had already put a call in for security, and that as soon as he stepped out of the bookstore, he'd be apprehended, but as he passed the front counter and the woman behind it—a woman he feared would be disgusted with him had she known what he'd just done—thanked him for stopping by, he knew that the only record of this would be the one written by his own personal recording angel, who might even now be weeping as the deceased waited outside the Piccadilly Cafeteria, wondering whether a sin that you planned to embark on could be forgiven if you planned the forgiveness ahead of time, when his mom finally appeared and said, "Did you find anything good?" a query the deceased would answer with a lie, saying, "No," and they'd continue their shopping, the deceased worrying that the page would fall out of his pocket, continuing to check to see if it was there, the page sticking to his fingerpads, later stashing it in a *CRACKED* magazine at home or inside a notebook or some other secret compartment, though eventually the guilt would become far too great, and he'd have to get rid of the photo altogether, wrapping it in newspaper and shoving it deep into the kitchen trash, praying that neither of his parents would lose their keys and have to resort to combing through the garbage, only to find this wadded up photo of a woman who, down to her last forty dollars, had been desperate enough to take off her clothes for money, who had followed the advice of the cameramen, who knew how to make women look as though they were the ones in control, as if this disrobing were exhibiting a kind of power that demanded the looker's absolute supplication

IV

here lies a man who spent his youth wondering if G-D had really used a man's rib to create a woman, and how could the Ark have contained all the world's animals, and how long did it take penguins to swim from Mt. Arat to Antarctica, had they simply migrated in the miraculous and impossible ways that animals inherently know how or had they been scooped up by the Hand of the Lord and deposited where they belonged, and was the wine that Jesus made from water actual wine or grape juice, and would masturbation truly make one crazy, and was it true that if the deceased entered a movie theater his guardian angel would wait outside and weep for his eternal soul, and speaking of angels, was there really one in heaven right now dipping a quill into some sort of cosmic inkwell and recording on the pages of a book bearing the deceased's name every deed he had ever committed and which Jesus Christ himself would someday read when he opened that book to see which of the sins the deceased had asked forgiveness for and which he had not, and how big was that book anyway, and how fast did the angel write, and did he or she document the deceased's every move, that is did the angel record in addition to the deceased's sins the everyday minutiae of cereal eating and waste elimination and tooth brushing and free throw percentages, and if there was a heaven would the deceased make it there, and how long was eternity, would he get bored, and were the crowns real or figurative, and what about those robes of light, was it true about what the deceased's father had said that G-D would never allow someone into heaven who would not be happy there, a notion that the deceased found perplexing since it suggested that G-D had constructed a particular kind of amusement park for a particular kind of people and if you didn't appreciate for example sliding down the necks of giraffes or skating on a sea of glass or worshipping at the foot of a golden throne then He would therefore banish you into oblivion, though not before allowing Satan to draft you at the End of Time into his army, which would attempt one last attack on the kingdom only to be incinerated by Heavenly Fire, some burning longer than others, each according to the extent of the evil in his or her heart, a time period the deceased hoped, supposing he had been predicted by the Father to be unhappy in paradise, would be for him short, which was admittedly an awkward thing to pray for: dear G-D please if it comes down to it let my agony be as brief as possible, may the fire that consumes me do its job quickly, may I have lead a life so that whatever evils exist at the moment of my final expiration be like a lightning strobe kissing the top of my skull, thus consuming me instantaneously amen

V

here lies a man who loved basketball, who had transformed his basement by nailing squares of wood to exposed beams and affixing Nerf goals to these squares and then sticking masking tape to the concrete floor to create a minia-ture court where he could re-enact Jor-dan's 1988 leap-from-the-free-throw-line dunk, a boy whose walls in his room shimmered with pages torn from *Sports Illustrated*: Jordan and Worthy and Magic and Herschel Walker and Tony Dorsett and Jordan again, because what human being could ever be cooler than Jordan, and why did white guys always look so unforgivably dorky in comparison, and who could possibly give the very least of a shit about the Frankenstein-like Kevin McHale or the bespectacled and spas-tic Kurt Rambis or the sparsely musta-chioed Larry Bird, a guy who was, like the deceased's father, shockingly—if not shamefully—pale, a player who seemed to have no particular style whatsoever, though of course he could get the job done, could clearly shoot, dribble, pass, knew the game, was fun to watch because you had absolutely no idea how such a klutzy-looking goob could make stuff happen, while Jordan—gleaming, aerodynamic, mischievous, innovative and endlessly improvisational—embodied a glorious and what-appeared-to-be-an-ultra-human superiority, a guy who could make leaping through the air—especially in slow-mo—look like the most amazing display of human athleticism, a phenomenon that was impressively imitated by a kid named Shawn, a black kid the deceased met at the Christian boarding school he attended for four years and who was twice as Jordan-like as the deceased could ever hope to be, since not only did he have some serious hang time but at 5'9 he could grab rim with both hands, a kid who was also an aspiring skateboarder and freestyler, who papered the cinderblock walls of his room with pages from *Thrasher* magazine, and began calling the deceased "Hoffman" for no other reason than he shared the name "Matt" with Matt Hoffman, the famous vert ramp BMX-er, and these two—

Shawn and the deceased—became inseparable, in part because they shared a love
of basketball and played it any chance
they could get, wolfing down plates of
cafeteria spaghetti in record time so as to
spend the better part of their lunch hour
playing one-on-one on an outdoor court,
and so it came to pass people began to re-
fer to the deceased as "Salt" and Shawn
as "Pepper," as the two were practically
inseparable, as they ate with each other
in the cafeteria, and cleaned busses under the instruction of the vice principal (a
squat little man with stubby fingers and
a shit-eating grin who reffed intramural
basketball games and called technicals
if you ever talked back or complained),
and gave each other surprise smacks in
the sack on the way to class, and listened
to N.W.A. on contraband Walkmans, or
engaged in impromptu wrestling matches, one of which—for reasons that would
later escape the deceased—got out of
hand, escalating to the point where
Shawn took a swing at the deceased and
hit him in the side of the head, and so
the deceased—his eyes now watering,
his mouth on the verge of blubbering—
swung back at Shawn and missed, and
did *not* have another chance to swing

again, as bystanders helped to break up the altercation, somebody saying, "Come on, you guys, make up, you're friends," which the boys agreed to do, perhaps somewhat reluctantly, nodding solemnly at one other, then performing a hand-shake that resolved in an authoritative finger-snap, neither of them knowing that this would be Shawn's only year at the school, and that they would not re-main friends or keep in touch, and that they would never see each other again, except—maybe—via cyberspace, the deceased typing the name Shawn and Shawn's last name into Google and click-ing the word "Image" and identifying a mugshot, a photo of a thirty-eight-year-old man who had been arrested for "fail-ure to appear in court," looking almost the same, except now a thin goatee orbit-ed his closed mouth, though his eyes—in this photo at least—were not the darting playful eyes the deceased remembered, the eyes here were squinting, nearly shut, as if—and it's possible the deceased was projecting, maybe even making stuff up—the man couldn't bear to see what the world had become, and though the deceased searched the web for informa-tion, for a way to contact this man who

had once upon a time been his dear and
even cherished friend, the only informa-
tion he could find was this "failure to
appear in court," a phrase that caused
the deceased to remember how, twenty
years before, the kid had never *not* failed
to appear in or on a different kind of
court, and that when he did, he often de-
fied the laws of gravity, how he—by his
own volition—had risen up and hung,
suspended—if only for a moment—
above the otherwise merciless Earth, and
how the deceased had been jealous, and
how he would like very much now to
talk again to his friend, to tell him that
he missed those days, and wouldn't it be
great, though they were probably too old
now, to get everyone together again—
the mulletted redhead from North Da-
kota and the buck-toothed guy with the
hook shoot and the entirety of the "Ko-
rean Posse" and the Indonesian kid who
never really knew what he was doing
but sometimes could bank in a prayer
and the Black Power guy who sometimes
wore a clock around his neck and those
Alabaman brothers who sported identi-
cal fades and the girl everybody thought
was a lesbian who could drain threes, etcetera & etcetera—so they could all meet

once more for one of those epic games of Twenty-One, where, even though it was every man or woman for him-or-her-self, a player always got recognized (usually with a congratulatory whoop, sometimes with a high five) whenever the ball, spinning and flickering on its lonely arc through space, swished home

VI

here lies a man who once befriended a
guy named Gary, a pale, skinny guy with
sideburns and a quasi-bouffant hairdo,
a guy who wore soccer shoes and jeans
and shirts bearing the emblems of German football teams, a guy who'd been
living out of his car and on the floors of
apartments rented by people he'd just
met, which included a girl from Nash-
ville who wore eye shadow and boots
and ragged t-shirts and smoked weed
and snorted Ritalin and kept a jarful of
prescription meds given to her by her father, all of which added up to the kind of
person who the deceased himself found
attractive and with whom he had seen
Pulp Fiction at a vintage movie house,
discussing afterwards the various plot-
lines while drinking fancy milkshakes
and finally engaging, at the doorstep of
her apartment, in a polite—if somewhat
awkward—kiss, the story of which the
deceased would end up telling Gary a

couple of days later, over beer and cigarettes, wondering if it had been stupid
to try to kiss her, or if she liked him, or
if she might be persuaded to like him, a
line of thinking that would cause Gary to
say something like, "Um, dude, I hate to
break this to you" or "there's something
you need to know," this something being that he, Gary, had recently had sex
(though he hadn't used the word "sex"
to describe what they'd done) with this
same girl, not because he'd particularly
liked her, but because she'd "come onto"
him, which meant that this girl was probably not the best girl to get involved with
and, truth be told, Gary had already
moved out of her place, had found an
apartment outside of town, a small, single room with one wall papered with a
scene from the Swiss Alps, a place where
Gary had lived quite comfortably until,
one evening, he'd experienced an allergic
reaction to a cigar he'd been smoking, a
cigar that had caused Gary's lips to swell
to epic proportions, though instead of
going directly to the doctor and finding
a solution for these swollen and apparently quite painful lips, Gary had stayed
up all night gazing into a mirror, watching his lips get bigger and bigger, star-

ing and drooling and laughing at himself and making stupid racist jokes, jokes that he repeated to the deceased when he called the next morning and asked to be driven to the emergency room, which the deceased did without hesitation because he considered Gary, who liked soccer and cocaine and typewriters and J.D. Salinger's use of dialogue and Pavement's *Slanted and Enchanted*, to be a good friend, even if he was also a mooch who smoked a lot if not at least half of the deceased's weed and often seemed to want to hang out *only* to smoke this weed and complain about how lame everybody else was, which, in the deceased's mind, somewhat regrettably, often rang true, since the famous college town where they lived was replete with hipsters and frat boys and sorority girls and lame-os who wanted to be in bands and play shows in the semi-famous venues in the college town where the deceased lived, a place that had recently been hailed the next Seattle by *Rolling Stone* magazine, a prediction which had failed and would continue to fail to come true, in part, the deceased liked to think, because no one had discovered me or heard of *his* band, a band that admittedly didn't exist and

never would, since the deceased knew
no other musicians except for this one
Jewish kid who played drums and loved
the band Rush, and let's face it, he didn't
know much of anybody, since, as a trans-
fer student living off campus, mostly in a
paranoid haze due to the amount of weed
he smoked, he had very few social en-
gagements and tended to only befriend
kids he met in writing classes, which
included the aforementioned writer girl
and also a guy who liked to drink bour-
bon and resent people who told him that
his writing sounded exactly like William
Faulkner (it did) and another girl who
wrote a story about a girl who, at the
story's climax, took off her clothes and
walked into a fast food restaurant and,
using the gun she was toting, blew a box
of chicken fingers to smithereens, and
then last but certainly not least there was
Gary, who loved music but did not sing
or play an instrument himself, though he
had once dressed up in an Elvis costume
he'd borrowed from his creative writing
professor, a man who'd not only written
a novel about an Elvis impersonator but
had also subsequently become an impersonator himself, as a sort of experiment
upon which, thanks to the urging of his

publisher, he had based a memoir, and so Gary, who already sort of looked the part of the King, what with his bouffant hairdo and sideburns, donned the costume and a pair of glasses and, cradling in his hand a billiard ball bearing the numeral 8 that he'd found on the side of the road, paid another guy who had purportedly raped a girl that Gary had gone out with a visit, a guy who, after he opened the door and found Gary, dressed as Elvis, on his stoop, had no idea what to think, could have in no way predicted that Gary would take the aforementioned 8 ball and smash in his nose, just bam, slammed the ball right into the guy's face, then turned around as the guy crumpled and, the deceased imagined, walked nonchalantly away, disappearing into the night, never to be seen again, which was par for the course as far as Gary was concerned, because it was Gary often met people and created chaos and then disappeared, leaving whoever he'd met to wonder whatever happened to that Gary guy, you know, you remember Gary and maybe the person who wondered about Gary would think, I'm gonna track him down, assuming he's still even alive, is probably still flying, as he has been known to do, under the radar, a guy who, despite his wit and charm and intelligence, might never have gotten it together, might never have ever come close to solving the mystery of who he really was, in part because he had never been able to get a straight or satisfactory answer about where he'd come from, a fact which the deceased personally knew to be true, as Gary had once told a story once about how, when he'd been rummaging around in the attic of his mom's house, he'd found a death certificate with his name on it and for a second he thought that he'd died or that this certificate was a prop that had played a role in some dastardly plot he had yet to uncover, until he finally realized no, this Gary the certificate referred to wasn't referring to him, the Gary this paper referred to was *another* Gary, a man who, it turned out, had been Gary's real father, a man his mother had refused, for all these years, to speak a word about, a man who, Gary eventually discovered, had drowned in a lake during a mysterious boating accident before Gary—the young Gary—could remember, a Gary that Gary had never in all his days known and never would, a Gary that might as well have been made up, a theoretical Gary that, for all practical purposes, might be said to have never existed, who could not be tracked down, and who had been reduced to a series of letters on a piece of paper, and thus remained forever unknown

and here lies a man who liked to imbibe
and often took it too far, a kid who had,
in his youth, smoked bags upon bags of
weed, a man who liked to get high and
who also liked to get low, a man who
liked, when it came right down to it,
to experience a shift in consciousness,
who liked to have his eyes dilated or
his central nervous system depressed,
who liked very much to feel euphoric
or to be clearheaded and sharp and en-
ergized, just as he liked to feel warm
and sleepy and fuzzy, a man who had
snorted crushed up Ritalin from the
cover of a Led Zeppelin box set in pitch
black eastern Washington, who had eat-
en a dope-laced brownie in Amsterdam,
who had smoked Northern Lights in the
mountains of southwest North Carolina
and failed to lead his friend to the wa-
terfall they wanted to view, who had
dropped acid and watched a Christmas
tree blink its candied lights as if receiv-

ing a holy and pleasantly indecipherable transmission, who had eaten mescaline and appreciated very much the ride he took in a Chrysler, which zoomed like a hydrofoil toward the heart of downtown Atlanta, a man who'd snorted coke off a tiny spoon in the bathroom of a famous restaurant in Cambridge and returned to his steak feeling magnanimous, who had tripped balls in Maine and watched as a sheet of gravel transformed itself into thousands of tiny skulls, a man who had stirred psychedelic mushrooms into applesauce and then went on a walk through the woods to stand at the edge of a lake and savored the sensation that he was an extraterrestrial creature visiting Earth for the first time, that is, until he heard in the distance the sound of a car horn repeating itself over and over, a terrible sound which not only ruined the pleasantly terrifying sensation of feeling like an alien but caused him to wonder aloud to his friend something along the lines of "who in their right mind would lack the foresight to turn off their car alarm, especially at a campground," only to subsequently realize that, in fact, the deceased was such a person and that the sound of the car alarm was com-

ing from his own car, a Nissan Maxima
that resembled (thanks to the fact that
its front was much longer than its rear)
a *Star Wars* landspeeder, but in any case
he high tailed it up through a stand of
pine trees, limbs smacking his face and
arms, tripping over fallen logs, arriving
at last at his car, only to find his other
friend who had not eaten psychedelic
mushrooms but had smoked enough pot
to be experiencing a complete and utter
freak out, which apparently involved
the misperception that the car, whenever
he tried to open its doors, was shock-
ing him and once they finally cut off the
interminable alarm, the deceased, who
was still very much under the influence
of psychedelic mushrooms, went around
to the other people at nearby campsites
and apologized and expressed how terrible that sound had been and that such
a sound, he knew, was the last thing
anybody wanted to hear after pitching a
tent in the woods, and after he'd made
his rounds he returned to stare somberly
at the campfire and watch the blinking
light of airplanes flying overhead like
UFOs skimming across the sky and was
subsequently struck with the notion that
the coals were sending him signals from

above like "Return to Me" and "Spread the Good Word," but it turned out that was just the comedown from the psychedelics, because the next day the deceased had woken and—though admittedly still embarrassed—felt exactly the same as he had the morning before, which is to say that he would very much like to find something else to eat or drink something that would transform his everyday feelings into extravagant ones

VIII

here lies a man who every time he took a
walk after dark in his neighborhood always and without fail asked himself why
don't you go for a walk every single night
of your life and what's keeping you from
doing this one simple lovely thing and
furthermore what's holding other people
back and why aren't more people out and
why in each and every home that is not
utterly dark does one always find at least
one TV flashing and why does the deceased care and why doesn't he look up
at the stars more often and acknowledge
the vastness of space and in turn medi-
tate upon his own relative insignificance
and subsequently feel blessed and lucky
to have beaten the odds of never exist-
ing and why doesn't he lay himself out
on the roof or build a little bedlike thing
up there where on evenings such as these
he might recline though let's face it he always knew that the answer to that particular question was that he didn't have

the necessary skills to build such a structure nor would it in a million years pass through the neighborhood's architectural committee which was one reason why he never built or paid someone to build that fence to safely enclose and combine his and his neighbor's yards and thus contain both the neighbor's dog which was half blind and totally deaf and left huge steaming loaves on the deceased's side of the yard and the deceased's dog who upon seeing other leashed dogs out and about with their masters often ran beyond the cul-de-sac and into the street where college students often peeled out and got pulled over by police motorcycles for reckless driving but it turned out that in this neighborhood of pea green or shit brown split levels the people had spoken and with one voice claimed to want to preserve whatever aesthetic unity these mold-encrusted houses with rotten trim could be said to uphold which meant that anytime anyone wanted to so much as apply a new coat of paint to their front door they had to submit for the architecture committee's approval a set of documents the effect of which was dispiriting and ultimately discouraged the building of such a fence so no fence was ever built and the dogs roamed as perhaps dogs were meant to roam somewhat freely if illegally and unsafely and furthermore no rooftop bed was ever put in place, and the deceased continued to forget to take walks after dark except on the occasions when he almost by accident found himself strolling through his neighborhood and if the stars were out he'd look and if the lights in his neighbors homes were on he'd stare wondering as he would continue to do as long as he lived why in the world didn't he do this more often and what besides himself was holding him back

IX

oh sleep in eternal rest man who once
drove from a town in Indiana to another
in Iowa so as to search for a place for his
family—his wife and his two-year-old
son—to live, and once he'd arrived at his
destination, and after following a realtor
to possible habitations, he settled (more
or less) on a craftsman-style house, one
with white exterior walls and blue trim, a
house that the deceased would subsequently—and, no doubt, stupidly—agree
to rent without his wife having had the
chance to see it—that is, by the time she
signed her name to the lease, she would
have viewed only the dozen or so photos
that the deceased had taken (using a
cheap and rather cumbersome turn-of-
the-millennium digital camera), a fact
that the deceased's wife would bring up
whenever she discussed the shortcom-
ings of this particular house, which
turned out to be quite often, since, from
the very first time she entered the house

she disliked it, not only because the rent-
al company had neglected to have it
properly cleaned, which meant that the
corners were coated with dirt and dust
and grime, but because it was, in many
ways, a house that had seen its better
days, a house whose basement utility
room was puddled with mud and standing water, which meant that if one wanted to keep one's feet dry during laundry
retrieval, one would have to walk from
the rickety and unsafe-seeming stairway
to the room where the decrepit washer
and dryer lived by following a series of
wobbling wooden planks placed strate-
gically along the floor, and furthermore it
was not clear whether the paint on the
front porch—or anywhere else in the
house, for that matter—had been the
kind produced with toxic lead, a chemi-
cal that—if ingested by their two-year-
old son—could cause brain damage and
lead to a host of other developmental
problems, but these things were only the
tip of the proverbial iceberg, as the family would soon discover that the floors
creaked and the loose window frame
whistled with cold air and many rooms
lacked overhead lighting and thus lan-
guished in various degrees of darkness,

and furthermore, every fall the house's bright white façade reflected the warm October sun, thus attracting thousands of ladybugs, who, thanks to the many cracks and openings in the house, found their way inside, releasing musky pheromones if you touched them or attempted to vacuum them up, which the deceased did on a number of occasions, not understanding that any interference at all with the ladybugs would trigger this aforementioned musk-release, thus attracting more ladybugs, and yet enduring this nightmarish plague of beetles—a swarm through which the family would have to travel whenever they entered or exited the front door of their house, squinting their eyes and batting the insects from their sleeves and hair—was infinitely preferable to the agonies the family suffered during the months of December through March, when the weather turned cold and damp and icy, and everyone pretty much stayed indoors, including the deceased and his wife, both of whom were working on projects that involved the consumption and organization and digestion and regurgitation of language, thus necessitating that they alternated who would be in charge of their son, one person taking mornings and another taking afternoons, and in this way a day or part of it would be "possessed," and so it came to be that in this family a person could be said to "have a morning," while the other person could "have the afternoon," and thus each spouse could lay claim to a portion of the day, and though this often seemed like an equitable way to distribute time, the deceased did not always, as the saying goes, use his time wisely, as he had never really figured out what to do with time, meaning both that he didn't know how to accurately conceive of it, like was it truly linear or was that a social construct, and furthermore time did not, for the deceased, pass by, as many claimed, quickly, and who, at a mere thirty-one years of age, thought if he were to pass on from this life to whatever awaited once his body was no longer animated (if, for instance, he discovered that he had cancer or if he died in a car accident or was brutally murdered) would probably think in his final moments that his life had been not only full but long, since he'd never known a time when he was not alive and so seemed always and eternally to have existed, and perhaps this accounted for his inability to use time (if time could be said to be "used") in an efficient way and thus perhaps his sense that he had "but world enough and time" accounted for how he might wake in the morning intending to write but instead checked scores and highlights from the previous night's basketball games or skimmed articles and the snarky comments left about boozy starlets or checked in with his family's slowly diminishing bank balance or read reviews of books by authors who had officially (and, for the deceased, regrettably) surpassed his publishing output, and by the time he finished checking up on things that absolutely did not require his attention he would often have burned through an hour or so of his allotted time and that part of the day would be gone forever, assuming you could say that time could go anywhere, which was, as far as the deceased was concerned, still very much up in the air, especially in the winter, when—for at least part of the day, and half of every weekend day—he had a two-and-a-half-year-old to entertain, which, during the summer, would've been fine because the deceased could turn on the sprinkler and let the kid run through it, or let him go to town with a plastic shovel in the patch of backyard where they grew tomatoes and jalapeno peppers, but in the winter, when it was 2 degrees outside with a wind chill of negative 15, with piles of dirty snow encrusted with sand and frozen rock-solid, you had to dream up excursions to other indoor places, which meant bundling up the kid and strapping boots to his feet then carrying him to the car, and driving to the mall, not the one in Coralville, because the children's museum there cost money and you couldn't go there without also visiting the carousel, which also cost money, but the one on the sketchier side of town, the one with the carpeted walkways and the Waldenbooks and the Ben Franklin hobby store and the toy library, where the kid could run around, his blonde curls—the same that allowed strangers to mistake him for a little girl—bobbing up and down, or maybe they'd go to the newly renovated public library, the deceased hoping that there wouldn't be like sixteen other kids fighting for the fake bacon and frying pans in the little toddler kitchen or that the line for the indoor slide would be short or that one Asian kid who liked to hog the caboose and the engine and hell all the other cars over at the train table wouldn't be there, and maybe once they got done with the library, they'd visit KIDSWORKS, a thrift store specializing in toys other kids had outgrown and where you could get a bag of old Happy Meal toys for a buck, a sack that the kid would be interested in for no longer than an afternoon, but still, an afternoon was an afternoon, and in one of these sacks—how many did they buy during their two-year stay in this town? who could bear to know?—there was a toy teapot, a representation of the same one that had appeared in a famous Disneyfied revision of a story titled "Beauty and the Beast," the film adaptation of which featured a host of anthropomorphic objects, one of which happened to be a chubby and haughty-looking kettle with an elephantine spout for a nose, and which the deceased used as a puppet, in part because his son loved nothing more than the occasions when the deceased made the son's toys talk, and which the deceased did from time to time, making the kid's life-size Curious George dance or poop or cover his eyes in shame, and all that was required of the deceased in order to create a satisfactory production was that he move a toy around while modifying his voice in some way, to make it very soft or very loud or very deep or very high or squeaky or nasally or whatever, and the kid bought it every time, staring at whatever the deceased was "making talk" with wide eyes, completely and utterly entranced by whatever narrative the deceased was creating, right there, on the spot, which, in the case of the teapot, hereafter referred to by the deceased and his wife as "Ms. Teapot," involved using a very high-pitched and—to the deceased's ears, anyway—aristocratically British accent, one that suggested that Ms. Teapot was accustomed to *harrumph*-ing, and what the deceased discovered was that, for some inexplicable reason, his son *did not like* the sight of this teapot nor the sound of the voice the deceased used when he addressed the boy, holding the teapot directly in front of the boy's face and saying things like, "Little boy? Have you been good today?" and "Have you been obeying your mommy and daddy?" and "I hope you won't disappoint me today, little boy," never using the son's name but instead always addressing him as "little boy," which had the effect of causing the boy to eye Ms. Teapot warily, as

he had clearly become worried by the el-
evation and the increased volume of her
voice and the way that she emphasized
all her points with a swift bob of her
nose-spout, and sometimes the boy became so concerned that his lower lip
popped out and so the deceased would
say, "Okay, that's enough, Ms. Teapot,"
and then he would return her to her
home on top of the refrigerator, and
sometimes the deceased felt guilty for
using Ms. Teapot at all, wondering if
maybe this time he had taken it too far, if
he shouldn't resort to puppeteering
when communicating his desires and
disappointments to a human being who
had yet to become a fully rational individual, and had a third party filmed the
deceased as he used Ms. Teapot, and
shown him the movie later, the deceased
would have surely been ashamed, as he
surely would've been after one occasion
in particular when, in attempting to convince his son not to cry, he described a
one Mr. Bojangles, an old man with a
gunny sack he carried should he happen
upon a child he could steal, a man who
could smell the tears of small children,
and there was nothing Mr. Bojangles
loved more than tears, and of course this

story was so gratuitously wrong in so many ways the deceased couldn't help but sort of wallow in its absurd but also horrific premise, which was not unlike the ghost story he told his son years later, after the family had moved to southwestern Virginia and had decided to camp overnight at a public campground, and how, a hundred years before, upon this very spot where they had pitched their tents, a boy named Issac had come camping with a group of kids, maybe a church group or a boy scout troop, but at any rate, before he left, the boy's mother told the man in charge that Isaac should not be allowed near the campfire, because he loved fire and would become so mesmerized by it he might walk straight into it, a warning the man in charge did not heed, as he figured the mother to be hysterical (as this was happening during a more-backwards time when men often thought such things about women, who they considered to be irrational and unreliable narrators of their own experience) and so night fell and the kids went to a nearby field to play capture the flag or hide and seek or some other game that would prove thrilling when played post-sunset, but Isaac stayed behind with the fire, and

sure enough, just as his mother had predicted, he became mesmerized by the
flames, and stared for so long at the coals
that his eyeballs burst into flame and
subsequently melted, which caused
Isaac—now a poor blind boy!—to become quite distressed indeed, and so he
ran off into the woods, where he became
lost, and eventually tumbled off the edge
of a cliff, where he died, and of course his
spirit still wanders these woods, a rest-
less and blind spirit who is looking for
eyes and who is carrying a spoon and—
not unlike the aforementioned Mr. Bojangles—a burlap sack, the former he will
use to scoop out the eyes of any little
boys and girls he finds awake after dark
and the latter to collect the actual eyeballs, because if there's one thing Isaac
can't have enough of, it's eyeballs, so
keep those peepers shut, my son, and do
not open them until it's daylight outside,
because as long as you squeeze your lids
shut tight, you won't have to worry, and
yes, it's absolutely that easy, please trust
your father on this one, he's the one with
experience here, he's lived long enough
to know that if you want to survive, just
remember this one rule of thumb: as
long as you keep your eyes shut tight,

absolutely everything will be fine

X

here lies a man who once stood beneath
an orange maple on a day in mid-Octo-
ber when the National Weather Advi-
sory had proclaimed that there would be
winds and low humidity and therefore
the perfect conditions for fire, and right
there above the deceased's head, on un-
dulating limbs, appeared the most extravagant flames, which, as the deceased
would like to admit, was probably a familiar metaphor for autumn leaves, but
what else could one think in the presence
of such incandescent scraps of orange
flapping wildly on black branches, while
smoky shadows pooled beneath and a
dog (not just any dog but one belonging
to the deceased's child, which was the
child's first and only dog, a dog whom
everybody—except those prone to pho-
bias or the generally heartless—loved
and who would be dead in probably
ten or so years if she was lucky but was
today very much alive) pulled eagerly

against her leash as the deceased walked up a limb-and-leaf-strewn street towards the place where Bus 127, piloted by balding and mirthful Gene, would soon perform the miracle it performed every day at more or less 3:50 post meridian, which was to deliver back to the neighborhood its children, who had gone away for the day to learn about treble clefs and subtraction and the Lakota Indians, who themselves believed that plants and trees like the one mentioned earlier had been sent by the benevolent spirit Waken Tanka to rise from the ground, the idea of which, along with everything else the children had learned, would be more or less forgotten once they streamed down the stairs of the bus and along the windswept lane with their heads shrieking and their arms flinging off coats and backpacks without seeing (despite their obvious glory) the trees, and certainly not saying (as the deceased had said on this day to himself): *I will be alive like these leaves only a short time longer, I will someday be carried away, I will turn to dirt and not know it, I will be gone and unable to return and whatever I have made will also expire and then I will be a flaming ghost in the heads of those who knew me and a mysterious face to those who view whatever photographs I leave behind and which some future person might view and wonder: did people really look like that back in the day, did they believe it was okay to dress like that, to make their faces look like that and who was this man and what did he do and what was his name and look how happy he was, look how utterly unaware he seemed to be of his own inevitable demise*

XI

here lies a man who, as a child, once
stepped on a copperhead and lived to
tell about it; that is, he stepped on the
snake and the snake failed to strike or
even move, an event that impressed the
deceased's parents, who claimed that the
deceased should thank his guardian angel, who'd apparently been on the look-
out and had spotted the snake up ahead
and, with his invisible arm, clamped shut
the mouth of the snake, which, after the
deceased's father poked it with a walking
stick, slithered away, disappearing into
woods that the deceased's grandparents
had recently purchased and would later
divide for their children, one of whom—
the deceased's father—would subsequently hire men to clear part of this land,
as he wanted to build a house there, and
these land clearers, during their labor,
would purport to have killed upwards of
sixty venomous snakes on this property,
and would assert that there was no land

in the whole county so snake-infested as
this particular mountain hollow, a claim
the deceased's father would prove whenever he happened to walk—in the cool of
a summer evening—around the perime-
ter of the house, carrying a walking stick
or a pair of snake tongs (a long rod with
a clamp at the end, operated by squeez-
ing a trigger on the handle), overturning
rocks and railroad ties until he'd found a
plump, crossbanded specimen—tongue
flickering, body flexing—which he might
catch and keep in a terrarium on the side
porch of the house, making trips to the
pet store two towns over to buy mice and
then watching with what could only be
described by the deceased as a sort of
morbid glee when the snake struck the
defenseless rodent, waited for it to stop
twitching, then unhinged its jaws and
swallowed it whole, a process that could
take a good fifteen to twenty minutes,
depending on the size of the mouse and
the size of the snake's mouth, which usually started at the head of the mouse and
worked its way down to the tail, a pale
and meaty extension that resembled, at
the end of the swallowing process, a very
long and slender second snake tongue, a
sight so horrific that it would cause the

deceased's father to laugh and would draw a disgusted hoot from the deceased's mother, who could not be said to appreciate poisonous snakes taking up residence on her porch, which meant that sometimes, upon finding a snake, the deceased's father would simply don the same brand of white plastic gloves he used when inspecting the mouths of his patients, remove the just-caught serpent to the driveway and behead it there with a shovel, afterwards razor-blading a body-long slit in its underbelly, peeling back the greasy sheath of its skin and fileting the body, so as to inspect its innards, to point out the still-beating bulb of a heart, and yank out the viscera, counting up—as the skinless body continued to writhe and whip itself lazily against the drive-way—the number of embryos it might be carrying, supposing it was female and pregnant, or slicing open the stomach in order to unravel the sopping remnants of a squirrel's tail or some other half-digested creature, all of which was deeply fascinating for the deceased's father, but only sort of fascinating for the deceased, who, despite having little interest in the study or vivisection of poisonous snakes, would, by virtue of living in this part of

the world, be called upon to kill them oc-
casionally, as he had on the summer day
when his mother had been dismantling
a woodpile and found a copperhead inside and therefore asked the deceased
to continue to search within this same
woodpile for more snakes, which he did,
and indeed there were more—four, in
fact—all of whom the deceased decapitated with a shovel, the blade rasping
against brick as he sawed back and forth,
attempting to cleanly sever the necks, the
bodies writhing long after the heads—
which continued to yawn menacingly—
had been severed, each of which the deceased scooped into a Ziploc bag to bury
later, because he wasn't sure whether he
should believe the old wives' tale about
yellow jackets sucking poison from dead
snakeheads and injecting a far more po-
tent sting upon their next victim, the
thought of which called to mind the time
he'd been clearing brush with his father
near the creek where he and his sister had
been baptized, and partly because the deceased had become tired and bored, and
partly because he happened to be filled,
on that afternoon and many others, with
preteen resentment, had plopped onto
the ground to rest and complain, only

to discover that he was being stung by a swarm of yellow jackets, and instead of realizing that he had dropped himself upon a nest—instead of getting up and *running away*—the deceased had writhed ineffectually upon the forest floor, that is, until his father scooped him up and jogged a short distance to the creek, whereupon he plunged the deceased's body into a pool and slapped the bees away, thereby saving his son's life, as there was no way to know how long the deceased might've wallowed there upon the nest, and whenever his father had occasion to recall that day, he would remind the deceased of this very fact, saying, in a playful and self-congratulatory tone, "I saved your life," a phrase that would replay itself over and over in the head of the deceased, along with other Dad-phrases like, "Always use protection," "Don't let your mother find that," "There won't be any liars in Heaven," and "We'll bury you," the latter of which the father uttered once during supper, after the deceased had asserted that he, as the eldest child, stood to inherit his parents' house and their snake-infested land, a claim that had inspired his father to suggest that he and the deceased's mother

would outlive the deceased, and therefore they would be responsible for digging his grave, the implication of which,
or so it seemed to the deceased, was
that the young man was perhaps living
his life in an irresponsible and probably
reckless manner, and though he figured
his father had been joking, this particular
phrase proved to have staying power, as
it had become one of a number of utter-
ances the deceased's brain had not only
recorded but looped and which he would
sometimes think about, partly because of
the way his father, who was an otherwise
unfailingly kind and generous man, had
said it, with the emphasis on "bury," as
though it were some kind of threat, and
though the deceased was aware that his
father loved him and would do absolutely anything for him, on other days he'd
imagine the shovel he'd used to crush
the necks of poisonous snakes breaking
open ground in the family cemetery, and
he'd wonder, as he always had, what his
father had really meant, and what he believed, and what was really inside the
head of this man who had a hand in the
deceased's creation, what thoughts and
dreams and premonitions the man would
always keep under wraps, what swarms

of unspoken things he, like the deceased,
would someday take to his grave

XII

here lies a man who loved outer space
and who, at age eleven, had listened with
rapt attention when an evangelist, whose
first name was Cliff (a man who appeared
to suffer from rosacea and whose head,
though not exactly fat, could definitely
have been said to appear swollen) presented a two-week lecture series about
how to correctly interpret the Book of
Revelation, what with its epic sideshow
of mutant beasts and harlots straddling
seven-headed leopards, all of which Cliff
the Evangelist and Amateur Astronomer
took time to decode, even shedding light
on the mysterious 666, which, he postu-
lated, was the exact number you'd get if
you added up the Roman numerals in
the name VICARIUS FELII DEI, which,
in Latin, translates into "Representative
of the Son of G-D," but which Cliff pro-
posed was the name of the first Pope,
and that this was significant because the
Catholic church had changed the day of

Christian worship from Saturday to Sunday, thereby consecrating a period of the week that was never meant to be consecrated, and that one day in the future, after the world had suffered plagues, perhaps initiated by nuclear war or some kind of environmental catastrophe or maybe simply the collapse of the world financial markets, an Antichrist would arise and perform miracles, and dupe those who hadn't spent time studying and *really* reading scripture into believing that he was the savior of the world, and that all that was wrong with the world could be cured by attending church on Sunday, after which laws would be passed that would force every person on the world to engage in Sunday worship, meaning that those who worshipped on another day would be put to death, but what these Sabbath keepers would know, because they'd read their Bibles, was that by worshipping on Sunday these misinformed people would be receiving, in their hands and upon their foreheads, the Mark of the Beast, while those who kept the true Sabbath would—in return for suffering persecution for obeying the Law—receive the Seal of G-D, and would be caught up with the Redeemed on the day when Christ returned, in a cloud of glory, ringed by angels, a sort of organic spaceship that would fly through the universe and, Cliff promised, pass through the Orion nebula, which, apparently, was a gateway to paradise, and though the parts of the seminar that depicted the possible persecutions of the Redeemed had filled the deceased with trepidation, he couldn't help but think, *Awesome*, whenever he imagined traveling on a cloud through space, though this idea began to transform as he grew older, especially after taking an astronomy course at a state university, where he learned about white dwarfs and black holes, and how, one day, the sun would expand into a massive red giant and swallow the Earth, a theory that was far less optimistic than the idea of riding a cloud through space to heaven, since, in this version, the dead stayed dead and nobody got rescued, and the universe, which was simply a place of light and dark and hot and cold, would continue on without humans, and that hadn't seemed too great, either, but then fast-forward about fifteen years to a time when the deceased had finished school and landed a job and formed a family and was approaching middle age, and one day, when checking his email, was surprised to discover a link sent to him by a dear friend who was well aware of his predilection for all things space-related and had correctly predicted that the deceased would be interested in listening to an album called "Symphonies of the Planets," which consisted of a series of recordings made by Voyager 1 and 2 as they were slung by gravitational forces through our solar system, logging massive amounts of data, including the interaction of solar wind on the planets' magnetospheres and trapped radio waves and charged particle emissions, all of which scientists later converted into sound waves, the result of which was a wash of strange ambient music not unlike something a couple of ragged-sweater-and-Converse-All-Star-wearing kids might make with tape loops on the floor of a big city art gallery, the main difference being that these sounds had been made by planets, which were, even as the deceased listened, still out there, still presumably emitting these same or similar transmissions, and it was as though the deceased had dialed into a secret radio station or was listening with a stethoscope to the heart of the universe, and so for days and then weeks as the deceased did the dishes and folded laundry and laced up his boots and donned a facemask and coat and gloves and went out into the bleak and snowy and frozen winterscape of his post-blizzard neighborhood, he did so with the symphonies playing through earbuds he wore and continued to wear even after they made his ears hurt, because listening to the symphonies had the almost immediate effect of transforming the mundane into the extraordinary, and forced him to acknowledge everything he saw as the product of energy and atomic particles, and for a moment he would feel as if he were an astronaut in his own house, the gurgling and the wobbling whistles and the static and the rumblings and the droning undercurrents and the bellowing and the wind-like screeches and the faint lonely ringings and the moan of what sounded to the deceased like lost human voices singing indifferently and perhaps unconsciously: it all made him prayerful and reflective, and even when the deceased wasn't listening to the symphonies, even after the battery on his MP3 player had been drained, he found himself hearing them in bits and pieces

when he least expected it, meaning that
he would become aware of doppler-
ing autos or the centrifugal whirring of
a neighbor's heat pump or the gurgling
and hiss of boiling potatoes and think
without irony or sentiment that what he
was hearing was indeed the timeless and
improbable music of the spheres

XIII

long no more for this man who exhibited a deformity called *pectus excavactum*,
meaning that in the middle of this boy's
chest there lived a hollow—or, as his best
friend insisted, a "dent"—with which
the deceased had a rather complex and
conflicted relationship, a random physical aberration that could not be blamed
on heredity, since neither the chests of his
father nor of his grandfathers exhibited
a place where the ribs curved inward
toward the sternum, a concavity that—
in the deceased's private moments—he
contemplated rather wistfully, in particular during bath time, when he pretended
his knees were big, swollen noses and the
dimples above them eyes and the length
of his femurs their freakishly long heads
and his toes their hilarious hair and his
penis some sort of eyeless slug that could
talk if he squished the head and thus
caused the pee hole to open, and if he laid
himself down and tilted his body so that

water ran across his chest, the bath-liq-
uid would collect in this aforementioned
dent, thus creating a pool where his toy
figures could soak their feet or his fingers
could splash, and in these moments his
chest wasn't something awful or ugly or
misshapen but instead had been transformed into a tiny oasis in the desert of his
body, where imaginary creatures might
recline and thus make the deceased feel
fine and good, which was not at all how
he felt whenever he had occasion to visit
the town pool, where, eyeballing all the
other chests without concavities, he realized that he would like, as the fat kids
did, to keep his shirt on while he swam,
as he feared his dent would be seen and
exposed and mocked, the possibility of
which touched the very soft and sympa-
thetic heart of the deceased's father and
caused the man to look into solutions to
his son's problem and lead him to discover a surgical procedure called the
Ravitch technique, which involved slicing open up the chest and peeling back
the flesh and breaking the patient's ribs
and sliding a titanium bar inside to keep
the bones aligned as they re-fused, a
process that would, if undergone, prove
extremely painful, and, in fact, the phy-

sician who would perform the surgery
explained that this Ravitch technique
was one of the most painful surgeries a
person could elect to have, and that the
recovery period would be quite lengthy,
involving as it would the re-growth of
those broken ribs, which moved every
time a person breathed, and much more
so when a person laughed or coughed
or sneezed, the prospect of which had
worried the deceased, but it seemed the
decision had been made, despite the fact
that the deceased wasn't sure whether
he was entitled to such a costly and in-
vasive procedure, especially one that
might be viewed by some as merely
cosmetic, since the deceased's dent was
not—as it turned out—that big a dent,
a fact he could plainly acknowledge
when the surgeon showed him slides of
other chests with incredible concavities,
chests that looked as if a giant thumb had
mashed a grapefruit-sized depression
into their ribcages, chests that looked
like they'd survived point blank cannon-
ball strikes, thus inspiring the deceased
to imagine the lungs and hearts inside
these chests competing for space, getting
all squished up in there, and here he was
with his puny little dent, a diminutive

hollow that could hold no more than one or two measley tablespoons of water, a dent those other chests would've probably killed for, but that he in his haze of self-centeredness had decided he somehow couldn't live with, imagining with trepidation a lifetime of reluctant shirt removal, but lacking the boldness to own his deformity, and figuring that the surgery was a foregone conclusion, he didn't try to stop his father from scheduling the procedure, and as the day neared, he donated pints of blood in case his future self should need it, and when the day came, he donned a smock, climbed aboard a bed with wheels, counted when the anesthesiologist instructed him to, woke up in excruciating pain, and spent three days in intensive care, where he would remember the following: the tremendous pain-blasts that accompanied being lifted off the bed for X-rays; the Mylar balloons and flowers and cards sent from his church and the church school he attended, all bearing messages imploring him to get well soon; the insanely beautiful blond nurse who—no kidding—gave him a freaking sponge bath, taking care even to swab his catheterized penis; his mom's friend Gracie who was loud and

72

obnoxious and made fun of him when,
because it hurt to speak, he would merely
whisper "ice" when he was thirsty, thus
causing Gracie to reply incredulously,
"who do you think we are, your personal
servants?"; and the doctor who came in
at the end and with no small amount of
bravado—in fact, with an Indiana-Jones-
type-flair—had yanked out the catheter
in a single quick whip; and how after the
deceased went home he had to use a plastic lung exerciser to increase base lung ca-
pacity, breathing deeply and holding the
air in for as long as he could, and sometimes when doing this his family would
make him laugh and it would hurt, and
in the end, he had no more dent but his
chest wasn't and never would be perfect-
ly shaped, because he didn't lift weights
or do pushups, and though he did try a
few times to exercise these muscles, he
simply wasn't inclined, didn't have the
heart or soul or will or whatever it was
that one needed to transform oneself into
the kind of person who would be completely and totally okay with removing a
shirt and baring one's naked skin to the
world

XIV

rest in peace man who at fourteen de-
parted his home to attend a boarding
school whose rules included no touching
the opposite sex and no exiting the dorm
after 7:30 pm and make sure you clean
up your room and make your bed before room check and attend chapel twice
a day and sing during song service and
don't eat meat and don't go to movies
and don't gamble or play dice or engage
in occult-type practices and don't swear
and don't wear t-shirts with double en-
tendre or t-shirts that promote rock and
roll bands and don't listen to rock music
because Satan, i.e. Lucifer, had once been
in charge of the music in heaven, had lead
the angels there in singing praises to G-D,
and don't you think that he knows after
six millennia of swindling human beings
out of eternal life what makes them tick,
meaning that if a song's not honoring
G-D, then it must be honoring the opposite of G-D, meaning Satan, a theory that
sometimes could apparently be proved

simply by asking the dorm chaplain to
fiddle with the auto-reverse feature on
one's Walkman, thereby allowing it to
play "Stairway to Heaven" backwards,
during which deceased heard quite clearly the phrase, "My sweet Satan, the one
whose little path would make me sad,"
a sentence which pretty clearly—at least
to the deceased at the time—laid out Led
Zeppelin's Satanic agenda, though the
act of hearing the lyrics in reverse didn't
exactly answer the question of whether it
was okay to play the notes of "Stairway
to Heaven" on one's guitar, as they were,
after all, just notes, not words, and therefore couldn't be said to "mean" or "promote" anything in particular, though
maybe if you played the notes you were
in some small but not insignificant way
honoring the song, but the deceased
put this out of his mind and continued
to play the notes of this and many other
songs whose purposes had—as far as he
could tell—little or nothing to do with
praising G-D, at least not directly, though
he figured that it could be argued that all
love songs, when sung sincerely, might
also be a celebration of the divine, a theory that the deceased's roommate—who
would, some years later, die of injuries

he sustained after having been hit by a taxicab piloted by a drunk driver in Korea, where he had been employed in the teaching of English—often struggled, as one day he—the deceased's roommate—would stare into the mirror and proclaim, despite the fact that his nose was way too big, that he resembled the lead singer of a new wave band he loved and the next he would chuck all his tapes into the trash or better yet burn them, imagining the whine and hiss and crackle of oxygen escaping and plastics melting were in fact the sounds that evil spirits were making as they left the cassettes, an idea that the deceased found rather preposterous, since why in the world would spirits that could conceivably go anywhere they wished or inhabit any kind of materials they wanted choose albums from the late 80s as their homes, why wouldn't they simply shack up inside a fourteen-year-old's body and ride it to the nearest bathroom, where, if that particular bathroom was unoccupied, that aforementioned fourteen-year-old might close his eyes and, taking hold of himself, imagine the face of the girl who worked as a grader of papers and tests for the school's pastor, who also taught several sections of Bible, a girl who laughed whenever the deceased came to visit her, which he had occasion to do, since he had been employed by the school to be the administration building's janitor, and thus had to wash windows and vacuum and replace urinal cakes and toilet paper and take out the trash in the pastor's office, where he often lingered, talking to the grader about the Beatles and Michael Stipe and R.E.M. and the Smiths and New Order and the Cure, the latter of which was the deceased's favorite band, and whose lead singer, Robert Smith—a kooky British fellow with pale skin and eyeliner and lipstick and black hair that he moussed into a ridiculous haystack on top of his head—the deceased idolized, going so far as to compose—during one of his monthly trips home—a fake news article about having been chosen to replace the singer and then finding a picture of the Cure band members as well as a picture of himself in which his head was the same size as the lead singer's, then cutting out a photograph of his— the deceased's—face and taping it onto the lead singer's face and making a photocopy of this on the copier his mom kept in the sunroom of their house so that she could print church bulletins, after which the deceased sent this fake news article to the boarding school's pastor's grader, who was impressed and amused, as she often was, and in turn this delighted the deceased, despite the fact that he knew this girl was out of his league, this girl who wore dark shades of lipstick and had droopy-lidded eyes and wore knee-high boots with skirts that were clearly too short, a girl who had a boyfriend in college who came to visit her sometimes on weekends, which meant that the deceased could not sit beside her during Vespers, though he did once ask her to a banquet, which the school held instead of dances—dancing being sexual and hedonistic and therefore dangerous—as did a guy named Sean, who lived off campus and invited boys over on Saturdays to play hoops in his driveway and watch R-rated movies, both of which would have been frowned upon by school administrators, as the seventh day of the week had been deemed holy and as such should never become a time slot wherein one participated in any quote unquote secular activity, but in the end the girl—who prided herself on being inscrutably unpredictable—said no to Sean and yes to the deceased, who rented a tux for the occasion of traveling by bus to a church conference center at a nearby summer camp, where the gussied-up students dined upon vegetarian lasagna and toasted one another with plastic flutes of sparkling white grape juice and watched *The Scarlett Pimpernel* or some other movie that would offend absolutely nobody's senses, and afterwards had their photographs taken in front of the conference center's fireplace, and on the ride back, the deceased had wondered what it would be like to kiss this girl, and though it seemed inconceivable, he prayed that she'd make the first move, that she'd think about rewarding him for having made her laugh and having presented her this evening with a Beatles poster (as it was customary to deliver to one's date a gift of some kind) and having purchased a boutonnière for her dress and spent over a hundred dollars on this whole banquet thing, but in the end, of course, the girl did not kiss him or place his hand on her breast and certainly did not come close to falling in love with him, though she did continue to write him mildly suggestive if not downright enigmatic notes (on yellow legal paper, with poor handwriting) during Pony Express—a Sunday night event that allowed boys to send notes to the girls, via a lucky mail carrier who was allowed to deliver them to the girl's dorm lobby, and for the girls to reply, their perfume-spritzed letters folded in extravagant and origami-like ways the boys could never reproduce—and the deceased continued to fall for young women who were out of his league, who wanted little or nothing to do with him, who claimed they didn't want to mess up their friendship because he was such a good friend, like a brother in fact, and though they understood that this news would disappoint him, they also made—as if granted with the powers of prophecy—a prediction, which was that someday someone—somewhere, somehow—would be lucky to have him, someday he would make a special someone very happy indeed, a sentiment that the deceased—who was prone to melancholy and heartache and skepticism, and who translated laughter and smiles and the occasional hug and even a friendly "love ya" at the end of a note as evidence of possible mutual affection—would always find difficult—if not impossible—to believe

XV

this grave contains all that was mortal of
a man who once hydroplaned on high-
way 76 through Hiawasee Georgia after
exceeding the speed limit in the rain the
car spinning in slowmo everything silver and streaks of ruby taillights the car
crossing the median and swinging into a
lane where the deceased braced himself
for the impending impact of an oncom-
ing semi he predicted would crush his
body to roadside jelly but suddenly the
car after having completed a three hundred and sixty degree turn came to a stop
in the middle turning lane facing the di-
rection he had been traveling and he had
no words for what had just happened except that it felt like a miracle like angels
had descended or the hand of G-D had
reached down and sideswiped him out
of harm's way and into the safety of the
turn lane no doubt about it this would be
something he would tell his grandchildren about but first he would type up

the story and send it to a youth magazine
distributed by his church and in the story he would talk about being the kind of
person who had not believed in miracles
and that once upon a time he would hear
stories like the one about the old woman who was sick during a megablizzard
and therefore unable to tend to her fire
or retrieve wood but then a tall stranger
appeared at her door and without saying
a word laid a fire for her and then went
away and once he'd left she'd hobbled to
the door and looked out and found no
footprints in the snow meaning that the
only probable conclusion was that this
stranger had to've been an angel sent by
G-D which before the hydroplaning inci-
dent would have caused the deceased to
roll his eyes but now maybe he had a different perspective only he sort of felt like
a phony after writing the story and even
more of a phony seeing it printed in the
magazine since this idea of a guardian angel had always struck him as somewhat
false because what about all the evil and
disasters in the world what about rap-
ists and predators and warmongers and
directors of genocide who'd unleashed
their wrath upon the innocent where
had their guardian angels been and was

it true that if the deceased entered a movie theater would his guardian angel stand outside the door and weep until he emerged which was something that the prophetess and one of the founders of the particular church he had been raised in taught because while he wasn't sure about guardian angels he was fairly certain that angels should they actually exist would not boycott theaters since what were movies but representations and who made them but artists and were artists bad and if so did angels stand outside the homes of artists weeping no the deceased thought he didn't think so or at least he hoped with all his heart that this was not so

XVI

this grave holds a man who, at thirty-two
years of age, made the executive decision
to renounce all barbers, to never again
give another human being legal tender in
exchange for the cutting of his hair, not
because he didn't enjoy the barber's cool
lather on his neck or the thorough sham-
poo supplied by a well-manicured hair-
dresser, but simply because a.) he'd
grown weary of styling his hair and b.)
he assumed that a more aerodynamic ap-
pearance would inspire him to exercise
more (it wouldn't) and c. there was no
good reason he could think of *not* to cut
his own hair, so out he went, to retrieve a
pair of clippers—a deluxe model that
vacuumed the clippings into a transpar-
ent, removable shell—and from that day
forward, the deceased became his own
barber, which meant that sometimes he
missed places and walked around with
chunks of hair longer than others but
also that, every two weeks, he popped a

number two guard onto the clippers and went to town, relishing the shearing of his head in a similar way to the satisfaction of mowing stripes across an overgrown lawn, thus establishing—over time—a uniform length—more or less—for all strands slash blades, and in this way the deceased was not only able to enjoy the gratification that so often accompanies the regular practice of personal hygiene, but also the satisfaction of a penny earned, since, by cutting his own hair, he saved himself hundreds of dollars a year, and furthermore, he began to cut the blond, cow-licked locks of his own son, an act that was—for this proud, self-taught barber—a touch bittersweet, as he knew that he was depriving the son of an experience that he had—once upon a time—dreaded, but now looked back upon as essential to his own social development, that being his trips, as a boy himself, to Parker's Barber Shop, which was run by a barber named not Parker but Mintz, a giant of a man who stood six foot six inches tall, wore size eighteen shoes, and would later develop (but not seek the removal of) a goiter the size of a grapefruit in his neck; a man who had to special order his scissors, because his hands were—like his feet—so large; a man who wore black, horn-rimmed glasses and a barber's smock whose V-neck revealed an abundance of salt-and-pepper chest hair; a man who could speak loud and laugh heartily but also knew when—for dramatic effect and for the purposes of encouraging young customers to sit still—to whisper, and though the deceased almost always dreaded getting his hair cut—mostly because it meant walking from his father's dental office after school to the shop by himself, and as a shy child he did not look forward to being in a room of strangers for any length of time—he would recall his time spent at Parker's Barber Shop with fondness, remembering the polished plum-colored leather of the chairs and the silver metal handle that, when pumped, raised or lowered the seat via a greased shaft; the glass containers filled with combs soaking in lime-green Barbicide; the mirror running the entire length of the western wall, where the letters of Parker's Barber Shop, which appeared backwards from inside the waiting room, reversed—and thus righted—themselves; the looped strip of hide hanging from the side of the chairs and which Mintz ostensibly used to sharpen his razors, though the deceased had never seen it used; the ancient cash register, its paint chipped; the heavy, vinyl-cushioned chairs: everything in the shop seemed to have been manufactured during a time when the idea of substantial mattered; that is, everything here was here to stay, everything here had committed itself to being around for a while, to not-changing, and therefore seemed somewhat strangely tinged with the pallor of death, as if entering the shop you weren't merely entering the past, but entering a place of dead-time, a kind of purgatory perhaps, and of course it made sense that in the hereafter there would be barbershops, after all, a person's hair would still be growing long after they died, an idea that always made the deceased think about the fact that all the dead people's hair he knew would still be growing, for how long he didn't know, maybe he should go to the library and look it up, "how long does hair grow after you die," though he knew he'd forget, at least until the next time he made it back to the shop, and the same thought entered his head, because the same thoughts always had a way of entering

his head here, the things of the barber-
shop were like symbolic talismans, calling up in one's head the same responses
each time, like, for example, when the
deceased studied the photograph of the
horse with six of Mintz's grandchildren
sitting atop its back, he always thought,
What a great blond beast, in part because it
seemed bigger than most horses, or was
it, he had no idea, or only a vague one,
not having spent time with horses, having been deprived of a life where one
harnessed beasts, to employ them for labor or pleasure, never knew the stink of
their steaming manure or the texture of
their hides, but at any rate, the deceased
thought this thought every time he entered this place, and thinking it made
him feel insignificant, like he had been
dispossessed of the kind of experience
that the men who came into this shop
gained, i.e., hunting and carving and cutting and loading and digging and hoeing
and working hard and long with their
hands and backs and legs, and when he
wasn't looking at the picture of the horse
he was looking at an outdated calendar
whose month displayed a cartoon of a
maniacal barber, who was shaving with
frenzied glee a stubbly strip down the

center of a terrified boy's head—a strange choice, the deceased had often thought, since many a child might've seen that picture and wondered "What if Mintz goes crazy" and "What if Mintz turns maniacal and shaves a strip down the center of my head" and "What if he makes me *bald*," though that was the thing, that was what made it work, Mintz was not crazy, would not ever go crazy, was too calm, too collected, and the fact that this picture hung on the wall, in a frame, no less, suggested that he was identifying the potential chaos that was hair-cutting, but also containing it, which, the deceased would later think, was maybe the way to go, to acknowledge the dangers of scissors and razors and make light of it, not with actual words but with a picture, so that the old men who came into the shop to talk about politics or the best place to pick huckleberries or the lack/excess of rain or the Japanese submarines that only the Elect know about and which live beneath Los Angeles or the old man who stuck a wild hog in the neck with a jackknife and held on till it bled out, all of which were stories that the deceased heard as he sat in the chair, worried what would happen if

Mintz were to become distracted by the details of one of these tales and snip a chunk of his ear right off, but of course that never happened, partly because Mintz had been cutting hair ever since WWII, when he'd shaved boys high and tight on an aircraft carrier, and partly because the deceased remained absolutely as still as he possibly could, a stillness he summoned only in this particular chair, a stillness that did not go unnoticed by Mintz, who used to tell the deceased that such stillness was the finest he'd ever seen, and who used to sort of not whisper but repeat "yes sir, finest I ever seen," and it did not occur to the deceased until years later, when he was cutting the hair of his own son—a kid whose skin was so sensitive that it would blush pink where the cut hair fell upon it, and who was not above pitching a fit in order to express his frustration about how irritated this skin had become—and he, like Mintz, whispered "be still" and then complimented the child on his ability to remain motionless, surprised to learn that Mintz's dramatic whisper, after all these years, had the power to subdue the bestial tendencies of his wild child, and so the deceased chanted it—"finest I ever seen, finest I ever seen"—an incantation that was so lovely and sweet and it deluded him into believing that when speaking to this child he—the father—would never raise his voice in anger again

XVII

to all ye who behold this stone let it be
known that beneath it lies a man who
did not want to take his son sledding at
the big hill because he was lazy and because it was two days after the big storm,
meaning that sledders had probably already shellacked the thing to greased ice,
not to mention that the storm had—in
its final hours—turned to sleet and now
walking through it was like stomping
through a frozen crust, not to mention
the wind chill was bringing the temps
down below any reasonable level, and
it wasn't that the man ended up having a change of heart as much as it was
that he'd become tired of his kid and the
neighbor kid begging and pleading, "can
we go to the big hill now, can we go to
the big hill now," the repetition of which
he needed to be saved from and so he
agreed and so they went dragging their
sleds and slipping on glassy patches of
ice on the snowy trails, which the boys

tried to sled on despite the fact that there were few places with a declension, which meant the man had to not only walk and stay upright with a leashed dog but also push with his boot the boys' sleds, and this took what seemed like an interminable amount of time, but when they finally reached the hill and the boys began to thrust themselves forward (lying stomach down on the plastic) the man smiled and whooped and allowed the dog who had been inside for a long time storing up who knows how much energy to run free and unleashed, bounding down the hill after the sledders then galloping back up, striding, as always, like a gazelle if gazelles were also friendly and wanted to lick and say hello to every stranger they ever met, a sight which the deceased had to admit he liked very much and would never have seen had he remained, as he was, inside his home in a house that, sometimes, had the effect of preventing him from experiencing what was outside, which was, of course, and always would be, life

XVIII

rest in peace man who, once upon a time
and in order to make ends meet, took
up the teaching of a class called "Public Speaking" at a Midwestern university whose main claims to fame included
having a train engine for a mascot and
playing host to highly ranked engineer-
ing and agriculture programs, the latter
of which had a lot to do with why the
communications department had insti-
tuted a rule discouraging the bringing of
animals or pets of any kind to class, since
there had apparently been problems
with students dragging hogs and calves
and/or ponies down flights of stairs and
into classrooms where they (the animals)
were no doubt as scared shitless as the
students whose charge it was to give a
speech consisting of little to no verbal
filler and effortless transitions and next
to no strange gestures, like the repeated
rubbing of an eyebrow that one corn-fed
redhead with a goatee had repeatedly en-

gaged in during his speech, but the thing was that one guy in the deceased's class had argued that his particular pet would be okay to bring because he could keep it in his pocket the whole time since it, as some species of Australian flying squirrel whose name the deceased would be unable to remember, was only the size of a finger, so anyway the deceased caved and the kid brought it in and the flying squirrel or whatever was terrified and would not for any reason let him or herself be pried with the kid's shaking fingers out of the kid's shirt pocket and so the kid went around to each student, bending over to let those who were interested peek inside his pocket, which was, of course, awkward and not so effective, since the shadow of the person's head who was looking in often obscured the little guy or gal inside, and though this was indeed embarrassing (as were many presentations) to watch, it wasn't nearly as bad as the time the smart ass who always sat in the back corner waltzed into class wearing a white karate outfit and asked a kid named Sam who always sat at the front of the class if he'd be interested in assisting him during his speech, to which the amenable Sam shrugged and said, "Sure," and stood up and allowed himself to be positioned in the middle of the room by this other kid, whose name the deceased has forgotten, but then the karate kid pulled from one of his suit's pockets a red and white box of Marlboro Reds, from which he slid a single cigarette, placing it between the lips of this Sam kid, making him look not cool at all, but in fact amplifying his inherent nerdiness and thus making him appear even more pathetic than he normally looked, but the smart ass was not through, he hadn't even yet begun to do his work, which was essentially a presentation that included an exhibition of his mastery of karate, and once it dawned on the deceased what exactly was transpiring here in the classroom of which he was supposed to be master, he winced but ultimately thought *surely the karate kid wouldn't try this unless he was a hundred percent sure he could kick the cigarette out of Sam's mouth*, though if the karate kid had been able to do so he certainly failed to exhibit that on this particular occasion, since, when he dropkicked the butt, he also dropkicked Sam's face, which immediately went red and as he adjusted his glasses everyone could see his eyes beginning to water, so he left the room while people were laughing and ooh-ing and ahh-ing and even though the karate kid apologized, the deceased had always suspected that he was far from sorry and that he had intended from the very beginning to kick the nerdy kid in the teeth, a theory, of course, the deceased could neither prove nor disprove and thus he would never know for sure what the kid had intended, only that he, as the one person who could have prevented the violence, had sat silently in a desk, and thus allowed it to happen

XIX

this stone marks the final resting place
of a man who, with his wife, had quote
unquote by accident created a child, at
least that's how they put it sometimes,
as if man and woman had been working
in a lab together and had blended vola-
tile chemicals without knowing what
the result would be, which, in this case,
was an infant with an oddly shaped
head and stuttered breath who lived his
first day beneath warming lights in a
neonatal unit, a situation that made the
couple uneasy, not only because it appeared that there might be something
wrong with the boy's respiratory system, but also because they'd been told
that the baby should, after having been
born, be handed immediately to the
mother, whereupon he might latch onto
her breast, and that if this didn't happen, the baby might encounter problems
down the road in terms of his ability to
breastfeed, a prophecy that, whether it

was self-fulfilling or not, turned out to describe part of the hardships of raising this particular infant, who, a few days later, the couple brought with them when they returned to their apartment on the main street of a lackluster Midwestern town, and though the child had seemed quite comfortable in the hospital, he now appeared to be very displeased if not downright unhappy to be alive, as if having been born was some sort of indignity best expressed in the arching of his back and releasing cries so anguished they would've seemed like parodies of an unhappy person had the two parents not been so terrified and sleep-deprived, and despite having watched the wife's belly inflate and pulse with life and having seen the child emerge from her body, it seemed like the baby had, like some sort of wild animal, come out of nowhere, as if they had simply gone to the hospital and returned with a very small, very displeased person, a person so discombobulated that one night, after what seemed like an eternity of trying and failing to calm him, the deceased—without thinking—had held the baby out at arm's length and yelled, "What is it that you want?" and then given the baby a shake, as if to get the point across—as if to reset him—but this only served to upset the child even more, though it did have the effect of changing the father's outlook on the situation, had woken him up, as it were, to the fact that he had done something he should not have done, and that he was a baby shaker, and that the "never never never shake a baby" posters had been printed for the benefit of someone like him, who, in a moment of weakness, might, after having unsuccessfully borne the shrieks of a deeply dissatisfied infant, done something he would immediately regret and which no ad campaign could have ever prevented, though, luckily for everyone, the deceased's son suffered no long term injuries, of that the deceased was almost completely certain, as this boy not only grew up to be strong and intelligent and even capable of outrunning the father during backyard soccer games, but also that he—that is, the son—had much more displeasure to express, many more tears to cry, while the father (sad to say) had many more things to yell and, not unlike a man executing feats of spectacular prestidigitation, many more failures to perform

XX

here lies a man whose life frequently
seemed as if its purpose were merely to
exhibit to his closest family members the
extravagant failures of his own character;
a man who lay in bed in the early morning hours thinking to himself that maybe—were he to remain absolutely still
for a few minutes longer—his wife would
wake and get the coffee started and thus
relieve him from the responsibility of doing so; a man who frequently disrobed
and, telling himself that he would pick
up his clothes later, merely left them
strewn upon the floor, where they lan-
guished for days in a moldering heap; a
man who often did not take his shoes off
upon entering the house and thus tracked
dirt (whether visible or invisible)
throughout the house and who failed—
despite having been asked time and time
again—to place his shoes on the rack
where they belonged; a man who bought
expensive or unhealthy foods that were

not on the grocery store list—or foods that, in fact, the family already had in their pantry or refrigerator; a man who failed, on occasion, to lift the toilet seat or—supposing he raised it—did not return it to its original position; a man who, though he loved his wife, barked answers at her when she made sensible and often necessary inquiries regarding the ways in which their day might unfold; a man who did not like to be disturbed, did not like to be asked trivial questions like "did you get the mail" and "what do we need from the store" and "what do you want for dinner," a man who did not want to be informed and did not want to inform others of his comings and goings; a man who yelled at his son because the son was behaving in a way that the man deemed ridiculous or annoying, even though—and in fact *especially* if—the son was mirroring behaviors—i.e., engaging in such acts as dancing, noise-making, nonsensical blabbering, or simply talking a lot—that he'd inherited from the father; a man who often ignored his family altogether and hid himself in his downstairs office, a place reserved for "writing" and "reading" and which the deceased used primarily to fritter away large portions of the day by visiting web sites that re-posted funny or ironic images and GIFs from other web sites, the viewing of which lessened for approximately two to four seconds the crushing weight of existence and the reality of his impending death, but of course this isn't to say that the deceased was always a total jackass, or that he wasn't capable of forethought or genuine charity, as he sometimes cleaned up after himself or surprised his wife and child with gifts, and neither was he always a such an epic waster of time, since, in order to remain employable he had to prepare lesson plans and grade papers and make up stories and send them out into the world, where, though some readers found his words acceptable and ushered them into print or online venues, most editors claimed his work wasn't "quite right" for the magazine or failed to fit their "editorial needs," responses that never failed to disappoint the deceased, who often attempted to quell this anxiety with a slowly-paced jog, an activity he often described to others as "running," which, honestly, was what it felt like to the deceased, who hadn't begun to engage in this sort of sustained exercise until he

was well past thirty years of age and discovered that not only did he feel better
whenever he ran upwards of three miles
but that once he got going, with the dog's
leash in one hand and in the other his
smart phone—which, with the help of an
application created by one of the world's
most famous manufacturers of athletic
shoes, would shuffle a playlist of anthe-
mic rock songs, thus making each mile
seem all the more triumphant, while also
recording his miles and the pace at which
he was running and the amount of calo-
ries he had burned, afterward using the
recorded voice of a famous basketball
player or tri-athlete or stand-up comedian to offer what the deceased liked to
imagine were personal congratulations—
he could enjoy the sensation of his legs
propelling him forward, of thinking
through problems like what should his
character in the current story he was
writing do next or how should he explain
to graduate students the concept of "the
rhetorical situation," and as his brain
carouseled through all these options, and
as the naturally-occurring endorphins
kicked in, the deceased would become
aware of how grateful he should be to
live on a street where he knew and genu-

inely liked everyone on his block, and in a neighborhood where he knew people didn't always lock their doors, and where miles of paved walking trails were kept up by guys in blue uniforms piloting golf carts with swiveling yellow lights on their roofs, and how improbable was it that he had grown up and gotten a job and married a stunningly beautiful woman who was much smarter than he and that together they had produced a talented and bright and healthy child, and that none of them had died or been seriously injured or contracted any debilitating diseases, and how—of all people he knew—he, the deceased, deserved this maybe the least of anyone, seeing as how he could, when he wanted, be a raging a-hole, and in these moments where he was aware that he was doing something good for himself for once and his lungs were burning and he could feel his pulse in his temples and the phone was pumping epic beats through his head he would become overwhelmed by the ephemeral nature of life and acknowledge that, at any time, any of these things could be taken away from him, thus turning him into a sniveling wretch of a person, and it should probably be noted at this point that while the deceased averaged a nine-minute mile and rarely went further than six (on his *best* days), he had also never once paused beforehand to stretch the muscles of his legs, since the deceased was by nature impatient, a man who had watched other runners engage in stretching exercises and thought, "Whatever" and "I don't need to stretch" and "I've never been hurt, so why bother" and "Honestly, stretching seems like a total waste of time," and so for a good long while he continued this line of thinking, until one day, a pang sang out behind his right buttock, a pang that continued to pulse with every step he took, and because the deceased was not the type of athlete who could, as they say, "play through the pain," and (truth be told) would not be remembered for his ability to tolerate pain of any kind—a fact to which his wife, who'd heard him on many an occasion release shouts so astonishingly loud that she figured he'd lopped off a body part, could attest—he limped into the office of a doctor who pointed out a problematic lump on his knee and, in addition to giving him the number of a man who made ergonomic shoe inserts for team members of the

Dallas Cowboys, encouraged him to make an appointment with a physical therapist, which he did, a woman who turned out to resemble a young, foul-mouthed comedian who made jokes about her vagina and poop and Jesus, none of which, it should be noted, were repeated by the therapist, as she was a self-professed Christian who explained body structure vis-a-vis the lens of why G-D made things the way He did and who, in order to ascertain the manner in which the deceased had been injured, commanded him to, "Show me how you normally sit" and "Show me how you normally stand," and so the deceased had showed her how he normally stood and how he normally sat, and lo and behold it'd turned out that he'd been sitting and standing the wrong way his entire life, and furthermore the therapist instructed him how and how not to stretch, ending each of these sessions by lathering the back of his thigh with a balm made of bee's wax and rubbing the base of his ass with an ultrasonic wand, inside of which, the therapist claimed, lay a crystal that sent vibrations into the deceased's body and broke apart the scar tissue, of which there was quite a lot, since all those years of quote unquote running had really taken their toll, which meant that if he wanted to get better he'd need to get a volunteer at home to rub his legs every night, so he'd gone to the pharmacy and purchased a container of "bag balm," a substance which had originally been intended to be slathered upon the chapped udders of cows but now the deceased would ask his wife to apply it to the backsides of his legs and his ass, and she would, with some reluctance, because she didn't like feeling the little bulbous bits of scar tissue and furthermore she was skeptical about some of the things that this therapist had said, having spent her whole adult life running and having once been the record holder for a track and field event at her high school, a fact that—while impressive—did not convince the deceased that she knew more than the therapist, whose stretches and wand-sessions ended up pretty much healing the deceased, though, when he tried to run for real, he realized how difficult such a thing actually was, that if he was going to try to emulate the proscribed form he would need to lengthen his stride, which meant he'd have to run faster, and though he could do this for three hundred yard stretches, he'd have to take breaks, plus it felt now like his other leg, or rather a tendon or muscle beneath his left buttock, was also starting to sing out in a similar kind of pain, and so, the deceased was forced to acknowledge that perhaps he possessed neither the will nor the ability to be an actual runner, though now, having been informed about the proper mechanics and form, he could point to the other runners he passed in his car and say to himself, in a rather judgmental and self-satisfied way that served to obscure his own jealousy, that none of them had any idea what they were doing, and that someday, these quote unquote runners would pay for—and forever regret—the mistakes they had made

XXI

here lies a man who as a boy would fol-
low his father into the woods and worry that he would be left behind because
what if his father wasn't actually his father but an android or a highly sophisti-
cated robot or even a sort of shapeshift-
ing alien which of course he was not or
so the son figured even though sometimes the idea took hold so fiercely that
the boy became nearly paralyzed with
fear for they were so deep in the woods
and so far from home and of course he
couldn't share this information slash fear
with his alien father who moved quickly
through the trees often allowing limbs
to slap backwards and hit the boy in his
face because if he did say something who
knows the alien father might have no
choice but to terminate the experiment
which was could two alien parents raise
two children i.e. the boy and his sister
without them knowing that they meaning the parents were aliens or androids

or whatever they were and yes of course this was only the result of a hyperactive imagination since in truth the boy's parents were kind and good and generous to a fault which was probably why the deceased entertained such thoughts in the first place since other fathers he knew had cheated on or divorced their wives because they didn't like them any more or because their wives had contracted degenerative muscular diseases and then these fathers had abandoned them for women who were not as nice or attractive as the first though maybe these second wives were better in bed a thought that would not cross the deceased's mind until many years later when he looked back upon a friend who was the product of quote unquote a broken home a friend who seemed from the perspective of the deceased to have the world as his proverbial oyster meaning that he was allowed to ride his bike wherever and whenever he wanted and who lived at his mother's trailer or his father's lake house or in an apartment behind his father's dental office which the deceased thought was incredibly cool not only because it had a light switch cover that featured a fat chef with his fly open thus granting the illusion that the light switch itself was a nubby penis one flipped up or down to magically create light but also because the deceased's friend was basically given full reign over cable tv and radio meaning he was allowed to listen to the album *Thriller* which had been banned in the deceased's home and to watch classic films like *Ghostbusters* which had also been banned in the deceased's home not only because of bad language but also probably because like *Thriller* both mediums presented the idea that the dead could come back and that there were such things as ghosts when in fact his parents and the deceased and his sister and his entire family going back for generations refused to believe thanks to their interpretation of the *Holy Bible* in ghosts or rather they believed that a ghost if you happened to be unlucky enough to encounter one was a manifestation of Satan who from the very beginning had taken the form of a snake and in order to convince Eve to eat from the Tree of the Knowledge of Good and Evil had promised that she would not surely die and thus the world's first lie would come to find itself reproduced over and over again in stories and song and this idea still rang true in the deceased's mind as he had to admit how tantalizing it was to believe in the supernatural or to even pretend to believe in invisible forces that were engaged in vast conspiracies which was probably what he was up to back in the woods trying to convince himself that his father was not who he claimed to be a man who ended up after many years of life to be a life form as familiar and alien as anything the deceased had ever known

XXII

and here lies a man who every week
cleaned who took out the trash who separated the recycling who organized his
waste who shaved who cleaned out the
sink after he shaved and cut his own hair
a man who mowed his lawn who raked
his leaves onto giant tarps and then
wrapped them like burritos and tugged
them onto the street where they rotted
for weeks before getting sucked up by
the city a man who hosed out his gut-
ters of dead rotting leaves that smelled
somehow of pig manure who swept his
porches who gathered the fading and
rumpled and mangled bats and balls in
the yard and returned them to their places or chucked them into the shadows of
shrubs bordering the yard who gathered
the dog's waste with either a plastic bag
by shoving his hand into it inside out or
by using a plastic hand clamp machine
that pried it from the grass and then deposited the waste into a bag a man who

dusted and vacuumed who rinsed dishes who folded clothes who let things get out of order then retrieved them who washed loads of laundry and folded his son's and wife's undergarments and their shirts and pants and shorts and towels and washcloths a man who dragged files into a representation of a silver wire mesh wastebasket that resembled exactly the one underneath his desk a man who took off his shoes most of the time before treading on the carpet of his home and felt guilty when he didn't want to waste the time to take them off especially when he knew he'd need to put them on again in a few minutes or even seconds a man who left footprints upon the stairs which he tried sometimes to erase from the carpet with his hands because he knew his wife didn't like knowing he'd walked on the carpet with his shoes on a man who lotioned his scalp to prevent dandruff and who dusted the dandruff from his coat shoulders a man who alphabetized his books who once separated his son's Lego bricks by color into plastic bags a man who sorted the recycling who shoveled ash from the mouth of his fireplace who made his bed who piled things up who stashed who became adept at hid-

ing what he didn't want found who
in the end will disappear and leave re-
mains to be dealt with and collections to
be gathered or distributed a man who
will someday be forgotten altogether
and who once found that to be terrifying
but now thinks it seems like a fire's light
slowly disappearing absolutely okay

XXIII

here lies a man whose son had wanted all
his life a trophy, the acquisition of which,
from the perspective of the deceased,
seemed strange, if not downright absurd,
in part because the deceased no longer
owned nor cared for trophies of any kind,
and the only one he'd ever won had featured a baseball player cast in cheap non-
precious metal, which had been screwed
upon a marble slab, whereupon a name-
plate appeared bearing the letters of the
deceased's name and the year 1982 com-
memorated the season he'd played reluctantly upon a T ball team named the DE-
MONS, a team that'd lost all its games,
except for the one the deceased had been
unable to attend, a team that'd featured a
chubby freckled redheaded girl who was
said to have grown into a strikingly beautiful woman, and a severely bucktoothed
kid who was said to have grown up to
become a crackhead, and though many
others also played, the only other person

the deceased could remember had been a long lost friend, who, according to his Facebook profile, had ballooned quite affably into the kind of overweight person that people describe as jolly and with whom you could expect to frequently laugh, even if this particular individual happened to make his living from an occupation whose description included the phrase "turf management," or, in layman's terms, the upkeep of golf courses, which, from an environmental point of view has no doubt catastrophic impacts on the land, though it's worth noting for those who have never had the pleasure of playing 18 holes that the sensory experience of strolling across a fairway in late afternoon or early morning is not unlike looking at a live version of those representations on felt boards in church school classrooms, the ones that depict Heaven and where the softly rolling hills appear always to be fastidiously groomed, suggesting that in paradise either angels are frequently employed in the mowing of grass or that the grass itself possesses a kind of intelligence and thus knows exactly when to stop growing, and all the kids there have robes of light and crowns with jewels, and in that awfully happy place one can expect that all this talk about trophies will have long been forgotten, as will the sorrows of a six-year-old boy with a flushed face and bright yellow hair, or, in other words, the deceased's son, who had trudged off the field at soccer camp sorry that he would not be bringing home a trophy, unable to understand the significance of the fact that his coaches had chosen him out of all the other kids in his age group to receive an award, not for the player who happened to get lucky and score more goals during the skill set drills (which was how one won a trophy), but because nobody in his age group during the whole week had outhustled him, no kid had tried harder, nobody had given more than he had, and yet the reality was that instead of a golden statuette this particular award earned the winner a tote bag and a Gatorade towel and a squeeze bottle, which, while certainly more practical, could not, especially from the perspective of a six-year-old, compare to the swoon-worthy gold of the trophy, which we must all admit is shinier and more impressive on a primal sort of level, and one is reminded of those birds (are they some sort of blackbird or raven?) who collect shiny things in order to lure their mates, or had the deceased merely been remembering that movie where the intelligent rats must escape the plow and so moved their house inside a hollowed-out brick to safety during a fantastic mudstorm, and ended up along the way befriending a blackbird with an eye for gold—or, as he said, "sparklies"—and in some ways, that's what it all comes down to: the refraction of light via metal, which is certainly a magical thing in itself, and which can never be said to be truly possessed, only experienced, but try explaining that to a demoralized and highly emotional six-year-old boy and see what he says and if, in the end, you can't sympathize with his point of view

XXIV

here lies a man who, as a child, spent many a Saturday afternoon riding in an orange Ford F150 driven by the deceased's father, a man with the softest of hearts and whose fear of causing anyone pain, coupled with his ability to sympathize with those who, for whatever reasons, had failed to take care of their teeth, meant that not only did it take him a good while longer than most dentists to administer an injection and remove a rotten tooth from an abscessed bed of gums, but also that he frequently did so without inflicting the least amount of pain, though that didn't mean he could be counted upon to pay any heed whatsoever to the "No Trespassing" and "Private Property" signs the family encountered whenever they explored remote mountain roads—ones that wound through shadowy coves and knee-deep creeks, past the houses of overall-wearing men who, reclining in pleather couches upon

their sagging front porches, raised with-
ered hands to wave—not because the deceased's father didn't believe in owning
private property but because he was as
curious as he was cautious, a trait that
would, in time, be passed down to the
son, who'd always admired his father's
willingness to more or less say, by ignor-
ing the signs and driving onward, "By
what right do you have from preventing
me from viewing this beautiful and otherwise cordoned-off part of the world," an
idea that might've resonated with those
native people our white ancestors had
rounded up and forced to march at bayo-
net point out of the mountains, a people
for whom the idea of fences, at first, had
seemed like an abomination, a people
who believed everything had a spirit and
that everything talked and if you sat qui-
etly and listened or asked a rock or a tree
or a stream a question you would—in a
manner of speaking—receive an answer,
since everything was alive, and who's to
say it isn't, in a manner of speaking, since
isn't every material object composed of
atoms, and aren't these atoms constantly
moving, and isn't that life, and furthermore, speaking of property, how could it
ever be "private," and how could land be

owned and who could soil or trees and water really "belong" to other than themselves, all of which were questions that the deceased couldn't help but ponder one moon-bright evening when he found himself playing Manhunter—a tag-slash-hide-and-go-seek-style game—with his nine-year-old son and his two nephews in a dark neighborhood in the suburbs of Charlotte, an otherwise unremarkable grid of townhomes bearing an insistently aristocratic name like Stonehaven or Woodleaf or The Chimneys of Marvin, all of which had been built to resemble miniature versions of Victorian homes, complete with gas-lantern-style street lamps and spires atop steeply-peaked roofs and front yards not big enough to spread a beach towel, and it was here that the deceased and his team—consisting of the deceased's son and the son's eldest cousin—had counted to forty and then soldiered into the darkness, to find and chase the other team, consisting of four boys between the ages of 11 and 13, the majority of whom had initially frowned at the idea of this obviously older (albeit hooded-sweatshirt-and-Adidas-wearing) man, would be playing Manhunter with them, until the youngest cousin vouched for the deceased, assuring the boys that he wasn't a creeper, just an uncle who liked to play games, and so the one group ran away to hide in whatever shadows they could find while the deceased and his group went looking for them, zipping between the houses that were oh-so-close to one another, the deceased thinking, whenever he glanced into the brightly lit townhomes, *you people with your lamps and your screen savers and your TVs ablaze with reality programming don't know what you're missing*, as there really was nothing more exhilarating—and, admittedly—exhausting, than chasing kids through the dark, in hiding and being chased oneself, at least until an old man opened his front door and barked, "Hey! It's okay if you guys wanna run around out here like chickens with your heads cut off, but don't go traipsing through people's yards, there's flowers and, uh, obstacles and stuff, so cut it out!" an utterance that seemed preposterous as it was 8:30 on an impossibly fine autumn evening, not to mention that there were, from the deceased's point of view, zero flowers or obstacles in sight, plus these Manhunter-playing kids, with their quickly thumping hearts, would not be kids forever, so the deceased spoke up and said, in a sarcastic tone loud enough for the old man to hear, "Yeah, you guys, stop being kids!" to which the old man, who had taken a step forward and, squinting into the dark, said, "Hey, are you the father?" to which the deceased replied, "I'm *a* father," to which the old man answered, "Well, you oughta know better than to let these kids run through people's yards," and "How would you like it if I ran through *your* yard?" to which the deceased, realizing now that he should set a good example for the kids who were watching, responded by saying, "I'd love it if you ran through my yard!," adding, "In fact, I'd totally welcome it!" to which the old man grumbled, "Well, keep them out of mine," to which the deceased said, "No problem," and the game continued, but the deceased didn't feel all pumped up or victorious, as if he'd vanquished a foe, only that it sucked that the whole neighborhood wasn't out here playing Manhunter and why couldn't everybody see that ownership was an illusion, that you were born poor and naked and that, unless you happened to be cursed with the wealth of Walt Disney and had yourself cryogenically frozen, you would no doubt die in the same conditions, so why not come out of your ridiculous Victorian townhomes, why not step out of—just for a night!—the illusion, why not have a world where we do not close our window blinds so that we can walk like the Dutch after dark and see into people's homes, why not during the summer and even into the fall do we not keep our doors unlocked so that kids playing Manhunter can take shortcuts, so that we can weave in and out of each other's houses forever, the streak of a human being running full-speed through one's home stabbing our hearts first with fear, then with the relief, as we'd remember that it was Manhunter night, and that the intruder was merely a neighbor, a person trying to get back to home base, to free the ones who'd been put in jail, so that the team could run away again, disappearing once more before their mothers shouted their names into the dark, calling them home for good

XXV

here lies a man whose father did not
drink, partly because he considered alcohol a health hazard, and partly because
his religion considered the consumption of alcohol to be sinful, and partly
because he worried what people in the
town where he lived would think about
him were he to place a six-pack into
his grocery cart, and partly because he
didn't trust himself, didn't think that he
could handle alcohol in a quote unquote
recreational fashion, which was a strange
if not inconceivable thing for the deceased to imagine, as his father was the
kind of man who had always seemed to
anticipate the desires of others and place
them before his own, a man who had often not followed up with those patients
who claimed they couldn't pay for the
bridge work or root canals or extractions
they'd just received, a man who served
on school and church boards, who spent
the weekends in winter splitting wood

for fires and in summer mowed grass, and who often became teary-eyed when standing before the pulpit in his church, pleading with parishioners to find it within their hearts to give money for the church budget or mission field, and yet this same man, who appeared to the deceased to be in control of every aspect of his life, would say, when the topic of somebody trying to quit cigarettes was brought up, that even now, after all these decades of not smoking, that he still had a desire to smoke, that the idea of it, of holding a cigarette between one's fingers and taking a drag and the ember glowing and then the long blue stream of smoke during the exhalation and the tapping of ash and that cycle continuing again and again until the cigarette had to be flicked away or smushed out in an ash-tray, was still in some sense seductive, but only in theory, as he knew better to mess with the likes of nicotine, often said things like, "you know, quitting smoking is almost as difficult as heroin," an observation that was never challenged by the deceased, who, in his youth, had sort of taken up smoking, albeit covertly, or so he'd thought, until the deceased's father approached him one day and said

he'd smelled smoke on the leather jacket
worn by the deceased, and that he understood the allure of smoking, appreciated
its mystique, and went so far as to claim
that—back in his own college days—
he'd experimented with cigarettes and
alcohol himself, albeit briefly, but that
whatever the deceased decided to do,
he should be careful, a warning that the
deceased—who'd been shocked that his
own father had ever so much as taken a
sip of alcohol, except for the near beers to
which he infrequently treated himself after working in the yard—translated into
a sort of endorsement for his own hedonistic lifestyle, since what was the next
cigarette or beer or whiskey dram but
an experiment, and as the years went on,
the deceased became more emboldened,
ordering beers in front of his parents,
and drinking wine at the parties of his
less conservative relatives, but then one
day, after he'd been married and become
somewhat gainfully employed, and after
he'd had a son of his own, he'd driven his
family from where they lived in Lafay-
ette, Indiana, to Chicago, Illinois, where
his father and mother were staying in the
Ritz Carlton hotel, not because they were
vacationing or even splurging, really, but

because the deceased's father attended every February a dental convention in the Windy City and the Ritz Carlton gave severe discounts to the dentists who had flown in from all over the country, and one night when everyone was lounging in the deceased's father's hotel room, the deceased's father asked the deceased whether or not he wanted to go for a walk, and the deceased said sure, so they descended in a golden elevator to the street below, and went out into the frigid night, the wind finding the cracks and chapping their cheeks, the father asking if the deceased had ever been to the Billy Goat Tavern, which the deceased had not, and so the father kept walking, as he always did, at a ridiculously brisk pace, frequently jaywalking and not seeming to care whether the deceased kept up with him or not, descending a flight of stairs and walking along a sidewalk that curved underneath an overpass, then it was into the brightly lit tavern, a place that seemed very much like a regular bar, with wood countertops and TVs, and the deceased's father asked the deceased whether he wanted a beer, to which the deceased shrugged and said, sure, and the father asked, what, and the de-

ceased told him, and the father ordered
the same, and they sat silently drinking
a beer together in this bar, the deceased
not looking at the father, and the father
not looking at the deceased, and later the
deceased would not be able to remember if they'd clinked glasses or not, only
that this was the one single beer that he
and his father had ever drank together,
and no explanation was ever offered, nor
sought out by the deceased, who knew
that this would never happen again, that
it was a singular experience, one that he
would return to now and again, unable
to penetrate what it might mean, and
never having the guts to say, remember
that time we sat at the Billy Goat Tavern
and drank beer like a couple of regular
guys, in part because he feared his father
might not remember, that he might claim
it never happened, which would mean
that the deceased had dreamed it up, a
scenario he could not bear, as he absolutely could not stand when, once you
came to the end, the narrator announced
that everything you had just read—everything in its entirety—had been nothing but a dream

XXVI

this stone here lies in memory of a man
who often appeared to have no memory,
who could be counted upon least of anyone he knew to relay phone messages
both important and trivial, who would
not say hello to his family if you asked
him to because he would not remember to
do so, who often forgot names of people's
children and who never remembered the
names of other people's pets, who forgot
to water the plants and lock the downstairs door before retiring, who forgot
where he'd placed his wallet and keys
and Swiss Army knife that he carried to
pare his nails and open objects that had
been encased in plastic, who often forgot
to submit bills on time, who left the car
windows down in the rain, who told stories to people that he had previously told
and who forgot the stories his friends
had told before, who missed meetings
that had been right there on his calendar,
who frequently—if you emailed him—

did not respond, who never once during the relatively short-lived era of video
stores returned a movie on time, who
paid enormous sums to libraries because
he had failed to bring back the books he
had borrowed, who often left his pants
unzipped despite having a fear of walking about with his pants unzipped, a man
who would have missed your birthday
had he known it, all of which adds up to
someone who—supposing we want to
put a positive spin on it—would totally
understand if you had forgotten who he
was and in fact promises that he will bear
no ill will toward you should you forget
him and, if, in the future, should the letters of his name in five ten twenty years
from now fail to ring a bell, rest assured
he would not be offended and would in
fact be more than fine knowing that his
name and face have completely escaped
you

XVII

here lies a man who often worried that
he was not spending enough time with
his son, that instead of kicking a soccer ball or teaching him not to double
dribble or how to play the theme to *Star
Wars* on the piano or showing him how
to properly reinforce his Lego starships
so they wouldn't crack apart the minute
anybody picked them up, he spent far
too much time in front of his computer
and phone, tinkering with words, reading and commenting upon his students'
papers, taking breaks to check scores and
read e-mails and log onto a virtual dash-
board that allowed him to scroll past the
images of all the blogs he followed, swip-
ing the mouse pad and positioning the
arrow on a valentine-shaped heart and
clicking it whenever he liked an image,
or the word "re-blog" if he wanted the
image to appear on his own blog, thus re-
serving with a curatorial glee the images
that had struck him as absurdly inexpli-

cable, like the toddler who was trying to light a cigarette or the couple lounging beside an idyllic stream while in the background a giant mound of raw strip steaks sat like a mountain of meat or the kid with a Darth Vader mask sitting alone and forlornly at restaurant table or a guy surfing past a wildfire or a woman sleeping in bed with an actual cheetah or a group of men shoving off in a giant canoe from an ice floe into what appeared to be a galaxy rich with star clusters or a man in a suit and a wrestling mask or a man wrestling a caribou by the antlers or a group of Mormon girls in dresses and braids playing basketball, all of which were mere confections the deceased used to distract himself from work, the computer becoming, as it were, a glorified "play pretty," a toy that allowed him to escape for brief moments the drudgery of daily life, if not to also suppress the fact that he had wasted, with the help of this infernal machine, an enormous portion of his only child's life, had probably dedicated more time to staring at its screen than he had staring at his own flesh and blood, who he could've taught—by this point in the son's existence—to do a great many things, but because he—the

deceased—was too lazy or impatient to
do so, the kid had not yet learned, for example, how to fold clothes properly, or
how to lift the toilet seat, or how to op-
erate a toaster, or how to spread peanut
butter on toaster waffles—two of which
the son had eaten every morning for the
last six years of his life—or use the pizza
cutter to slice these toaster waffles into
bite-sized squares, and, furthermore,
the deceased, as a teacher of English,
could've overseen the correspondence
between his son and all manner of pen
pals, could've played piano alongside
his son instead of yelling at him to practice a quote unquote actual song and not
to bang please, could've created persuasive incentives for his son to identify and
memorize the names of leaves and trees
and birds and animals and flowers in his
neighborhood, could've shown the boy
how to plant seeds and fertilize plants,
how to start and maintain and stoke and
feed a fire, but the sad truth was that the
deceased, despite being employed by a
state university, often felt crippled by
what he didn't know and had failed to
accomplish or learn, as he was, when it
came right down to it, a man who could
not change the oil in his car or remem-

ber what the word "hypotenuse" meant or explain how the stock market worked, neither could he—following a total collapse of the economy and societal systems—be expected to subsist upon the bounty of the natural world, could not track and kill an animal and roast its meat on a makeshift spit above a fire he'd built without matches, could not read the night sky except to point out the two most obvious constellations, a man who had never put together a piece of furniture right the first time, because he simply could not bring himself to read the instructions before proceeding, a man who did not floss frequently enough, was not—sad to say—always a friend to animals, a man who wondered if the world into which he flung this message would look back on his generation and say thanks for nothing you heartless bastards; thanks for continuing to bring people like yourselves into the world; thanks for getting suckered into buying bottled water; thanks for making cheese-flavored corn chips and crack cocaine and candy bar nougat and strips of dried steer muscle and strips of processed cow teat secretion; and thanks for carrying this quote unquote food away in plastic bags that blew away and subsequently made their way down creeks and into rivers and then the ocean, which carried them to a place where all the world's plastic bags had gone, thus forming a huge monstrous plastic soup, which, when it nudged against a continent, barfed out a thick, gooey sludge; thanks for spraying your lawns with chemicals to kill the grubs and dandelions; thanks for buying all those slabs of liquid crystal, which relayed images of helmeted barbarians, the majority of whom died young and forgotten but nobody cared because a parade of new and better gladiators were always rising, rising, rising; and thanks people who demanded wars to avenge their enemies even though their enemies couldn't with much precision be identified; thanks people who sent their sons to these wars because their fathers and grandfathers had gone before them to wars of their own; and though the deceased could go on he would rather say he's sorry, because he too used aerosol canisters of lubricant to ensure that food wouldn't stick to the pans in which it cooked; he too was a champion of refrigeration; he drove when he could've walked; he depended on others to grow his food; he spent hours staring into screens watching fat guys lip synch to Moldavian songs and busty babes biting their lips and orangutans peeing into their own mouths; he too sucked at the electric teat of Appalachian Power; he too dreamed about getting off the grid but instead clung to it for dear life and with the full knowledge that someday there would be hell to pay—but then again, someday the sun would expand into a red giant and swallow the earth, and you couldn't do much about that, either, except maybe, at the very least, when your son, on a late fall day, asks you to throw a ball in the back yard, you might, for the love of all that's holy, put down whatever it is you think is more important, bobble the poorly snapped ball, and, as you dodge invisible defensive linemen, tell your son to go long

XXVIII

this stone marks the final resting spot of
a man whose grandparents purchased
one hundred acres bordering National
Forest in southwestern North Carolina,
where owls and whippoorwills and wild
turkey and the lesser-seen wild boar
roamed, where springs bubbled from
the underneath mossy folds in the earth,
where ferns turned gold in autumn,
where streams pulsed with trout and
crawfish and water snakes, where trails
lead across bridges of hand-hewn wood,
through rhododendron thickets that
could be twilight-dark at midday, and up
steep inclines and past rugged boulders
scabbed with crisp fungi and through
groves of pine trees and along ridgetops
where you could gaze westward toward
Tennessee and view the mountains re-
treating into the distance like green-blue
waves, and one of these trails passed by
a clearing that'd been designated the
family cemetery, a place where the de-

ceased's grandfather had first been laid to rest and then after him the deceased's grandmother and also the deceased's grandfather's two sisters, one of which was adopted, but neither of these sister's graves had been marked with official tombstones, which seemed to the deceased problematic, if not plainly wrong, though his father didn't appear to think so, as one of the sisters had been adopted and another, in his view, had been not so nice, and apparently this not-nice-ness had deemed her unworthy of an official tombstone, which, as already mentioned, the deceased found troubling, since both great aunts were, after all, family (and what's more human beings), and yet they'd only been granted, like the three dogs who'd been buried at the deceased's grandfather's feet, a creek rock to mark where their final resting places, a fact that inspired the deceased to wonder what kind of stone he should have and should he get it ahead of time or should he leave instructions as to what words should be engraved upon it, if only to make sure it was done right, or did he even want a stone at all, why not simply have one's body burned and then sprinkle the ashes, or, supposing one happened to be concerned about the carbon monoxide emissions and other contaminants and thus one's final ecological footprint, especially where cremation was concerned, maybe one should consider the process of alkaline hydrosis, which dissolves a human body into a fine white powder and which is unfortunately illegal in most states, despite the fact that cemeteries are overcrowded and funerals involving traditional caskets are overpriced and environmentally unfriendly, and that they interfere with the natural processes of the breakdown of cellular organisms, and besides who would want to have their blood drained and replaced with chemicals and be transformed by someone into a morbid doll, a question the deceased would ask periodically, despite the fact that he knew the answer, which was that in many situations this practice provided a great deal of comfort for survivors, like say a girl's been raped and had her head's been bashed in but then a mortician comes along and puts her back together so that her parents can see her one last time and say goodbye, an example provided by the mortician and poet Thomas Lynch, who penned a memoir about how he believed in making dead people look presentable, an argument the deceased found quite compelling but not ultimately persuasive, since it'd always bothered him to stand before his grandfather's grave and imagine not that the man's dead body had dissolved into the teeming storm of molecules beneath his feet but instead had simply only *sort of* dissolved, the idea of which would cause the deceased to wonder if his grandfather's casket had been properly sealed, and if so, did that prevent his suit from slowly deteriorating and had the preservatives worked, and what would it mean for them to have "worked," and would the deceased's grandmother, who died more than two decades after her husband, be a leg up on him decomposition-wise, since she had gone into her grave wrapped in a quilt and placed in a pine box, as requested, having had the foresight to plan ahead, which again reminded the deceased that he should let whoever reads this know to please make sure that the deceased has been properly cared for, would you perhaps take the time to inquire if his headstone in fact bears these words, and if his body has been prepared in a way as to truly be food for worms

XXIX

here lies a man who, on a day when the
wind was blowing—gusting, as they say,
at forty-five miles per hour—was nearly
blown off his bicycle, the same one he'd
owned for sixteen years, which meant it
was only two years younger than some
of his students, which meant that they
were oh-so-young, so young in fact that
the majority of them failed to retrieve
troubling memories when asked to write
about where they had been on September 11th, not because they were so young
they couldn't remember the event, but
because they had been middle-schoolers
in middle school classrooms, and these
classrooms had been managed by terrified middle school teachers, who feared
what would happen if they allowed the
students to watch the fantastically hid-
eous footage, to see living symbols dis-
integrating before their very eyes, like
some gifted CGI animator's nightmare
of what life would be like in the future,

though now, ten years later (which, for everybody back in 2001, could've technically been categorized as "the future"), buildings are not falling, at least not today; today, we have 3D aliens in the theater and higher gas prices and tablet computers and bedbug infestations and sports figures who imagine women who are not their wives will be impressed by photographs of their genitalia, and a new Chipotle, where, on its opening day, people lined up for hours because they believed the first customers would get free burritos for a year, and the deceased was sorry to say (but perhaps not too sorry) that he too went to this same restaurant, he too stood in a long line with his fellow townsfolk and waited in a smallish room furnished with stainless steel tabletops while loud and unidentifiable rock was piped into the space where customers watched Chipotle employees rolling up enormous burritos, the contents of which, according to a sign overhead, might or might not have their origins in the nearby countryside, a concept that caused the deceased to acknowledge that this was the age of Worrying What Might Happen If We Don't Make Better Choices, and that future generations

will remember us by the ways in which
we worried, how we were told to worry
and we did, how we were told to do exercise and conserve electricity and how
we intended to but then we procrasti-
nated and then we just plain forgot, but
we weren't all bad, or at least we liked to
think we weren't, since, didn't we stand
over our children at night and sing songs
because they asked us to and we always
gave in because we knew they would
only ask for so long someday they would
not want us to sing our grandmother's
songs someday they would want to be
alone they would want us to go away
and we would and we will and we will
be missed, and then forgotten

146

XXX

at your feet rests a man who would, were
he present, like to know why you are here,
why you have come, how is it that of all
words you might read you have chosen
these, and what is it you expect to learn or
understand, what do you hope to gain by
eyeballing the rambling meditations of a
man who is and who will be for all practical purposes once you read this gone,
why would you care about a stranger you
will most likely never meet, what does it
say about you that you would submit to
such a relentless onslaught of verbiage,
who are you, what do you know, why
are you still here, not that you shouldn't
be, not that the deceased doesn't find
the idea of you still being here after he
has said goodbye somewhat comforting,
though he hopes your stay will—in some
way, shape or form—elevate your spirits, supposing you even believe in spirits, if not then treat yourself to whatever
indulgence your conscience—if you still

can be said to be in possession of such a thing—will allow, and take some time to reflect upon the fact that you have eyes or, supposing this has been, in the unlikely event, translated into Braille, that you have fingers or, supposing a famous actor is reading this and you are listening (also unlikely but not unpleasant to imagine), that you have ears, whatever and however it is that you are receiving this message, please ask yourself what would you say if you knew you only had maybe five or six more breaths before dissolving into oblivion, would you say "Sorry" or "I love you" or "I never loved you enough" or "Tell so and so they are forgiven" or might you simply save those words for yourself, preferring, as would the deceased, to ride out silently with the studio of your head resonating only with those last draughts of air and in that head a silent countdown to expiration: five breath four breath three breath two breath one breath zero

Matthew Vollmer

Matthew Vollmer is the author of *Future Missionaries of America*. He is also co-editor of *Fakes: An Anthology of Pseudo-Interviews, Faux-Lectures, Quasi-Letters, "Found" Texts, and Other Fraudulent Artifacts*. He teaches in the MFA program at Virginia Tech.

CPSIA information can be obtained
at www.ICGtesting.com
Printed in the USA
LVOW07s1215311217
561408LV00002B/317/P